THE ART OF PEACE

THE ART OF PEACE

◆

*Nobel Peace Laureates Discuss
Human Rights, Conflict and Reconciliation*

José Ramos-Horta, East Timor

Betty Williams, Northern Ireland

Dr. Rigoberta Menchú Tum, Guatemala

Archbishop Desmond Tutu, South Africa

President Oscar Arias Sánchez, Costa Rica

Harn Yawnghwe, for Aung San Suu Kyi, Burma

Bobby Muller, Co-founder, Intl. Campaign to Ban Landmines

Jody Williams, United States

His Holiness the Dalai Lama, Tibet

◆ ◆ ◆

Edited by Jeffrey Hopkins

Snow Lion Publications
Ithaca, New York

Snow Lion Publications
P.O. Box 6483
Ithaca, New York 14851 U.S.A.
Telephone: 607-273-8519
www.snowlionpub.com

ISBN 1-55939-149-9

Library of Congress Cataloging-in-Publication Data
The art of peace : Nobel peace laureates discuss human rights,
conflict and reconciliation / José Ramos-Horta...[et al.];
edited by Jeffrey Hopkins.
p.   cm.
Transcript of the Nobel Peace Laureates Conference
on Human Rights, Conflict and Reconciliation held at the
University of Virginia, on Nov. 5–6, 1998.
ISBN 1-55939-149-9 (cloth)
1. Peace—Congresses. 2. Human rights—Congresses.
3. Nobel Prizes—Congresses. 4. Pacifists—Biography—Congresses.
I. Ramos-Horta, José. II. Hopkins, Jeffrey. III. Nobel Peace Laureates
Conference (1998: University of Virginia)
JZ5538 .A78 2000   323—dc21   00-008436 CIP

 PRINTED IN CANADA

Contents

From left to right (*standing*): Harn Yawnghwe, for Aung San Suu Kyi, Burma; José Ramos-Horta, East Timor; Jody Williams, United States; His Holiness the Dalai Lama, Tibet; President Oscar Arias Sánchez, Costa Rica; (*seated*): Bobby Muller, Co-founder, International Campaign to Ban Landmines; Dr. Rigoberta Menchú Tum, Guatemala; Archbishop Desmond Tutu, South Africa; Betty Williams, Northern Ireland. *Photo by Bill Clark.*

Preface

Bringing Together Great Hearts and Minds

Sometimes it may seem that beings on this planet have reached their present state through survival of the fittest—and among the fittest, perhaps the most fierce, the most capable at combat. However, even more has been achieved through cooperation, through friendship, through care and concern. We have found that no matter how coercively force is structured, it achieves limited and shaky results.

Also, sometimes it may seem that happiness depends solely on economic success or failure. However, to a greater extent happiness depends upon the morality of cooperation, friendship, care, and concern. We have found that even though a modicum of economic success is essential, it is not sufficient for happiness.

Two types of experiments—one focused on state control and another focused on unbridled greed—have run their course; these have shown that without respect for human rights, conflict inevitably arises, thereby undermining the very control and economic development that are sought. Power and money—when not constrained from within each person out of a concern for others' rights—eventually turn against themselves, undoing the benefits for which they were pursued.

While many who strive to bring the world into balance work in relative anonymity, several have received international recognition for their selfless efforts. Such is the case with the nine great hearts and minds who convened in Charlottesville at the University of Virginia for the Nobel Peace Laureates Conference on Human Rights, Conflict, and Reconciliation on November 5 and 6, 1998, presented by the University of Virginia and the Washington-based Institute for Asian Democracy. These activists shared with the world and with each other their views about the importance of recognizing basic human rights, their concerns about the conflicts that arise when these rights either are not perceived or are denied, and their ideas for achieving reconciliation. At the core of their agendas is the conviction that morality is essential for personal, political, social, and economic balance. They believe that without a personal ethic that includes compassion for other beings, mere self-concern will eventually undo the fabric even of one's own life.

José Ramos-Horta of East Timor calls on us to recognize the right to self-determination, especially in territories that have been annexed by other nations. He notes that such people are treated as expendable and traces this attitude of negligence ultimately back to ignorance. Lack of knowledge of what is marked out as "other" leads to prejudice and then to distrust and fear. The result is that people in these areas are sacrificed for pretended pragmatism. The solution is in dialogue, discussion between communities.

Betty Williams from Northern Ireland brings into vivid perspective the effective force of women and children to readjust the priorities of the world and stop conflict and war. Stemming from her wish to protect her own children from destruction by a society bent on making the littlest suffer, she calls for action based on caring motivation. She movingly provides us with a Universal Declaration of the Rights of the World's Children, asking that we pass beyond compassionate tears to action.

Dr. Rigoberta Menchú Tum of Guatemala emphasizes that indigenous peoples use conversation and dialogue to solve problems and can serve as sources of inspiration for an intercultural world. She calls for us to value the rights of indigenous peoples for our own good and insists that we recognize their rights so that they can break free of stereotypes that lead either to silent ghettoization or to patronizing overprotectionism. Legal patterns built on the assumption of a homogenous people need to be amended to take account of the multivalent cultures within nations. Hers is a voice ringing with respect for diversity.

Archbishop Desmond Tutu of South Africa eloquently makes a case for restorative justice, for reconciliation upon sincere public recognition of past misconduct, restoring harmony. Celebrating God's creation, he emphasizes our incredible capacity for goodness, despite a capacity for incredible evil. He advocates avoiding revenge on the one hand and blanket amnesty on the other and provocatively makes the case that, with true acknowledgment of guilt, the healing power of forgiveness makes retributive justice neither necessary nor helpful in certain transitional situations. (For a full account of his views and work on the Truth and Reconciliation Commission, see Archbishop Tutu's *No Future Without Forgiveness,* published by Doubleday, 1999.)

President Oscar Arias Sánchez of Costa Rica presents an alarming host of facts and figures that document the ridiculous waste of money and resources in arms proliferation—the warped mentality that seeks profit out of exacerbating poverty. His methodical presentation of misplaced priorities and disproportionate wealth rings with the power of a reasoned, compassionate plea for economic reform. He warns of the rapid changes inflicted by a pattern of globalization based on greed and speculation, rather than on human need. Advocating an International Code of Conduct on Arms Transfers to regulate and monitor weapons sales, he calls for reorientation toward human security, which is founded on concern with human life and dignity, appreciating diversity, and stressing education.

Harn Yawnghwe, participating on behalf of Aung San Suu Kyi of Burma, presents a brilliant, step-by-step analysis of the obfuscating formulation of the amorphous camps "East" and "West" and the misuse of this concept by certain Asian politicians to suggest that Asians are not committed to human rights. He shows that, at its origin, the Universal Declaration of Human Rights actually had strong support from smaller countries in the third world and that the notion of supposedly different "Asian values" was seized upon by Asian dictators as an excuse for repression. He documents how democracy and human rights are not at odds with actual Asian values and patiently draws us to realize that there are universal aspirations to democratic principles, specifically in Burma.

Bobby Muller of the United States, co-founder of the International Campaign to Ban Landmines, which was a co-recipient of the Peace Prize, contrasts Archbishop Tutu's presentation of restorative justice with the deterrent value of retributive justice. First telling his own story as a marine volunteer for the Vietnam War, becoming disillusioned with the war, and after being wounded, becoming disgusted with Veteran's Administration hospital care, he inspiringly describes the persistent long-term process of promoting legislation to ban landmines. He gives insights into the importance of individual initiative and the vagaries of trying to change entrenched attitudes.

Jody Williams of the United States, drawing on long experience with the worldwide effort to ban landmines, speaks with a gripping call to action. Describing a new model for activism based on the globalization of citizens' movements, she emphasizes the need for coalition members to respect each other's independence within working cooperatively. Activists should work consistently and intelligently to dissolve the barriers of distrust between government and civil society on issues often considered by government to be beyond the purview of ordinary citizens. Warning that governments can be disrupted by this new mode of activism, she calls for maintaining the persistence of nuts-and-bolts drudgery and never falling into the trap of sentiment without action.

His Holiness the Dalai Lama of Tibet concludes the conference with a moving description of the need for a compassionate motivation and the need for knowledge of long-term consequences of actions, especially the negative effects of violence. He calls for "inner disarmament"—moving beyond the concepts of "we" and "they" and narrow-minded nationalism in an interdependent world in which one's own and others' welfare are intertwined. Compromise is the only solution for the contradictions inevitably occurring in a diverse environment, and concern for others is a way to open one's own horizon and gain strength. Observing that the human race has become more mature, he suggests that we set as our long-term goal global disarmament, stressing that through hope and determination the seemingly impossible can be achieved.

With a clarion call, these nine great hearts and minds insist in concert that:

- knowledge needs to undermine ignorance
- compassion must dissolve intolerance
- coordinated activism has to replace passive acceptance and despair
- dialogue must transform recrimination
- innovative justice has to displace vengeance
- morality needs to supplant emphasis on the bottom line in commerce and law
- recognition of universal rights must unseat disenfranchisement
- determination over a long period of time is required to overcome entrenched forces
- transformation of motivation must accompany action.

By organizing this conference and publishing the presentations, I hope to encourage attention to and discussion of these topics. It is my hope that by witnessing these conversations by and among the Nobel Peace Laureates, and through probing and absorbing their meaning, we will be stimulated to reflect on the often complicated and difficult implementation of attitudes and techniques for peace.

The idea for the conference originated in discussions with Michele Bohana, Director of the Institute for Asian Democracy. My relationship with His Holiness the Dalai Lama, and Michele's relationship with Betty Williams and with other Nobel Peace Laureates led us to speculate about the provocative results of bringing these and other laureates together to discuss their ongoing work for peace. I subsequently shared our idea with Raymond J. Nelson, who was then dean of the College and Graduate School of Arts & Sciences. Nelson embraced the idea and presented it to the president of the University, John T. Casteen III, in September 1996. Two days before Christmas of that year, the three of us met, and President Casteen committed significant initial funds from his own office. I then took a proposal for the conference to the Page-Barbour and Richard Lecture Series Committee, which supplied the majority of the funding.

Of the twenty-one living Nobel Peace Laureates, we invited several whom we knew had participated in group efforts before. One such effort had taken place in Thailand on behalf of fellow laureate Aung San Suu Kyi of Burma; a second group effort had taken place in New York to establish a code of conduct on arms transfers. We also invited the previous year's Nobel Peace Prize recipients. Nine of the eleven laureates we contacted were able to accept our invitations.

Melvyn P. Leffler, the new dean of the College and Graduate School of Arts & Sciences, was especially helpful in providing logistical support and in suggesting the names of eleven professors to develop an educational lead-up to the conference. This group produced a series of sixty lectures, panel discussions, and films at the University of Virginia and other Charlottesville venues from September to November, 1998.

More than twenty University of Virginia staff members, representing areas too numerous to list, were also crucial to the success of the conference. This group literally made everything possible. I was continually amazed at their expertise, good humor, volunteerism, and flexibility in working across departmental lines. At the center of these various activities was the untiring contribution of our always effective conference coordinator, Bryan Phillips. This Ph.D. candidate in Religious Studies, suspending work on his dissertation, played a crucial role in making the conference a reality.

As I see it, the aim of all the hard work by the administration, faculty, staff, and students involved in this conference was to provide an atmosphere for provocative conversation among the Peace Laureates on the stage of Old Cabell Hall Auditorium. The aim of that conversation was communication to the audience in the Hall and to many others through simulcast transmission at the University, through cable transmission in the Charlottesville area during and after the conference, through satellite transmission over North America, through Internet transmission, through broadcast and rebroadcast by C-SPAN, and through distribution by the United States Information Agency to 130 countries. The aim of that communication is to stimulate individuals and groups to reflection on and discussion of agendas for peace. The aim of that reflection and discussion was implementation of techniques that will effect a diminishment of suffering.

I feel that the aims of the conference are fulfilled when persons— anywhere in the world—become inspired from even a single statement and strive to alleviate a level of conflict and pain. There is more than a good chance that this will happen, since these laureates have, over a long period of time, striven in the face of difficult odds to achieve a measure of peace and thus have spoken with the wisdom of experience and heartfelt conviction. They speak with their whole being.

The Political Liaison to the Laureates and Organizational Advisor was Michele Bohana, Director of the Institute for Asian Democracy. The short biographies of each of the laureates were composed by Kathleen D. Valenzi. The transcript of the conference was prepared by Steven Weinberger.

The conference was sponsored by the President of the University of Virginia, John T. Casteen III; the Dean of the College and Graduate School of Arts & Sciences at the University of Virginia, Melvyn P. Leffler; the Page-Barbour and Richard Lecture Series at the University of Virginia (Chair, Daniel J. Ehnbom, Associate Professor of South Asian Art History); Dr. Inder and Vera Vaswani Chawla; Terrence D. Daniels; PMD International, Inc.; Wallace Stettinius; and CFW Intelos.

With wishes for stimulating inquiry into the sources of our conflicts and of our highest ethical aspirations,

Jeffrey Hopkins
Organizer and Director, Nobel Peace Laureates Conference
President, Institute for Asian Democracy
Professor of Religious Studies, University of Virginia

NOBEL PEACE LAUREATES CONFERENCE

Human Rights, Conflict and Reconciliation

Presented by
The University of Virginia and
The Institute for Asian Democracy

Remarks by Melvyn P. Leffler

Dean of the College and Graduate School of
Arts & Sciences, University of Virginia

It's most fitting that this historic gathering should take place here on the grounds of the University of Virginia, an institution founded by Thomas Jefferson. He was one of the country's first great statesmen. As minister to France, as the first secretary of state, as the third president of the United States, he was a tireless advocate of peace. He believed that rational dialogue rather than brute force, and self-determination rather than imperial domination, produced the most enduring and just solutions to national conflicts and human aspirations. Peace for Jefferson's young republic meant progress and enlightenment. Peace promised prosperity, happiness, and the moral improvement of humankind. Peace allowed for the cultivation of all that was noble in human nature and the suppression of all that was brutish and benighted. Peace reflected the victory of rationality; war, the triumph of unreason. Peace was the hallmark of civilization; violence, a vestige of barbarism.

Mr. Jefferson's hopes for an enlightened world order have been sorely disappointed. Reflecting on the last hundred years of war and genocide, the carnage appears almost incomprehensible. But understand it we must, because the world today is, in fact, a violent landscape scarred by civil strife, ethnic hatreds, arms races, and persistent struggles for liberation and self-expression. During the last decade alone, over four million people around the globe have been killed in violent conflicts. Approximately one in every two hundred persons in the world today is a refugee. Countless others suffer under oppressive political regimes that deny fundamental rights to the individual. Millions of people remain victims of undeclared wars, vicious rivalries, and traditional patterns of racism and ethnic hatred.

The end of the Cold War has distracted the attention of Americans from the world around us. Without an ideological foe, without a perceived threat to our interests, without an evil empire to challenge us, our concerns and our energies have turned inward. Armed conflicts in other countries appear less relevant. They are viewed as isolated incidents. They become a part, not of our history, but of others' history. In the post–Cold War era, we must not allow our interests in peace, stability, and human liberation to erode. We must not allow ourselves to become indifferent to the suffering of fellow human beings engulfed by war, famine, and ethnic hatred. As recent events in the former Yugoslavia illustrate, local conflicts are not without international ramifications. We must not forget that domestic peace is closely linked to world peace; that today's regional conflagration can easily become tomorrow's international crisis, engendering talk of armed intervention and the deployment of troops.

But military intervention must not be our first nor our last resort. The threat of force may bring combatants to the bargaining table. Lasting peace, however, requires dialogue and the construction of norms and rules for more rational national behavior. Consequently, we need to try to understand the sources of national conflict, as well as the reasons for ethnic and racial strife, arms races, and institutionalized patterns of domination and subordination. But we must also go beyond analysis of past events. Historical understanding is not enough. Our real challenge is to imagine enduring solutions. This conference presents such an opportunity. The University of Virginia has the honor today and tomorrow to host a group of men and women who have not flinched in the face of adversity, cruelty, prejudice, and senseless violence. Their presence here should catalyze our own interest in the study of conflict, the pursuit of peace, and the quest for human dignity. Indeed, this conference illustrates our conviction that we must educate ourselves to understand the language, the sources, and the meanings of peace and human reconciliation if we are to avoid the horrors of war and the degradation of the human spirit. And this conference should also remind us that peace is itself a learning process, an ongoing struggle for understanding and for enlightenment.

It is now my great pleasure to introduce one of the organizers of the conference, Michele Bohana. Michele Bohana is director of the Institute for Asian Democracy, a Washington-based non-profit organization. She has been absolutely instrumental in bringing together these great hearts and minds, and it is an honor to have her here today to help inaugurate this extraordinary event.

Remarks by Michele Bohana

Director, Institute for Asian Democracy

For the next two days, we will be partaking in a dialogue with some of this era's leading advocates of human rights, open societies, and the rule of law. These individuals have witnessed what ensues when human rights have been trampled upon, when the results of a free election are annulled or ignored, when self-determination is an unrealized aspiration, when indigenous peoples suffer the consequences of forced cultural assimilation, when weapons of mass destruction remain unchecked, and when weapons of war, landmines, continue to pock our earth and maim our brothers and sisters.

They come to this university, the expression of Thomas Jefferson's manifold vision, to discuss the underlying theme of this conference: Human Rights, Conflict, and Reconciliation. The Universal Declaration of Human Rights was adopted and proclaimed by the General Assembly of the United Nations on December 10, 1948. Thereafter, December 10th became known as International Human Rights Day. The document itself contains thirty articles that enshrine principles which uphold fundamental freedoms protected by the rule of law. It declares that "member states have pledged themselves to achieve, in cooperation with the United Nations, the promotion of universal respect for, and observance of, human rights." It is *prescriptive*—it is what we as individuals, as nations, and as a community of nations *should* do to protect the inalienable rights of all members of the human family.

What occurs when the principles enshrined in the Declaration are violated? What transpires when human beings are denied justice, freedom, and their inherent dignity? Ethnic and regional wars become far more likely. Conflict occurs between citizens and ruling governments, between societies, races, and creeds, and, on a smaller scale, even between families. Anger, frustration, and hatred supplant reason, compassion, and kindness toward others.

The conflicts human rights violations produce are often precursors to disease and famine affecting men, women, and, sadly, children. Conflict is often accompanied by fear. It is the freedom from fear and want that is proclaimed in the Universal Declaration as the highest aspiration of the common people. The right to think, to worship, to make political choices freely, is in harmony, not in conflict, with peace and prosperity. That is the central insight of the Declaration, and possibly the most clear lesson of this past century.

Regrettably, it is a lesson that must still be taught. In an article published recently by *The Washington Post* entitled "Pinochet Case Signifies Cries for Retribution," a young Holocaust survivor is quoted as saying, "This century has been stained, *bloodstained*, from the beginning. The Armenians. Hitler. Stalin. Mao. Pol Pot. Bosnia. The Kurds. The Chechnyans. The Algerians. The Kosovars. And of course the Jews." The Department of State's Annual Human Rights Report, and corresponding reports of Amnesty International, Human Rights Watch, and Freedom House are weighted with page after page of detailed human rights abuses resultant from the abuse of power and unresolved conflict.

These laureates, exemplars of the human spirit, have shown us that it is possible to overcome the most deeply rooted and entrenched systems of repression in Ireland, South Africa, Central America, Tibet, Burma, Guatemala, and East Timor. They have campaigned against landmines, the weapon that continues to disfigure and kill long after conflicts are resolved.

But such people do not come our way often, and that reminds us that getting into conflict appears to be a whole lot easier than resolving conflict, and resolving conflict through non-violent, peaceful means is more difficult still. And so, over the next few days, we will examine conflict. How, then, does one resolve conflict?

Does reconciliation contravene the notion of legal retribution? What about international human rights laws, war crimes tribunals? The international community has determined that crimes against humanity are subject to universal jurisdiction.

It is the hope of the conference organizers that by bringing together great hearts and minds we will enhance our understanding of the question our topic raises. To be on this stage in the company of Bishop Tutu, who finds in his heart the ability to forgive even the system of apartheid, and offer reconciliation to those who give voice to their unspeakable crimes in a public forum—all predicated on the belief that forgiveness heals—makes me examine my own sense of morality. One may consider his appearance here, and that of his peers, as a *teaching*. We *need* teachers, we *need* to listen deeply and integrate inspiration with aspiration. We need to practice what we learn, and to integrate the important lesson from *these* teachers into our daily life.

I wish to take this opportunity to thank the University of Virginia and its sponsors, and all UVA staff for their tireless efforts to make this conference a success. I would be remiss if I did not acknowledge the contribution of Bryan Phillips—our detail man, the conference coordinator; and Jeffrey Hopkins for his cherished friendship and vision of a more peaceful world.

I will now turn the proceedings over to Julian Bond. He is a professor of history here at the University of Virginia. He is also chairman of the National Association for the Advancement of Colored People, and I don't think we could have found a more able moderator.

Opening Remarks by Julian Bond

Professor of History, University of Virginia
Chairman, National Association
for the Advancement of Colored People

It is my high honor to be the moderator of the sessions today and tomorrow. May we all stand for a moment of silence in memory of those who have lost their lives in the struggle for peace.

Thank you. I want to very quickly introduce the speakers in order of their receipt of the Prize:

- Betty Williams of Northern Ireland—honored in 1976-77 for her grassroots work that began the Northern Ireland Peace Movement.

- Archbishop Desmond Tutu—honored in 1984 for his Campaign for Truth, Justice, and Peace.

- Oscar Arias Sánchez—honored in 1987 for helping bring peace to Central America.

- His Holiness the Dalai Lama—honored in 1989 for his efforts to help create a free and democratic Tibet.

- Harn Yawnghwe, representing Aung San Suu Kyi—honored in 1991 for her work to bring democracy to Burma. Harn Yawnghwe is director of the Euro-Burma Office in Brussels.

+ Dr. Rigoberta Menchú Tum—honored in 1992, the youngest person, for her work in fighting for the rights of aboriginal people.

+ José Ramos-Horta—honored in 1996 for his work in seeking freedom for East Timor.

+ Jody Williams—the co-recipient of the 1997 Nobel Peace Prize for her efforts to ban landmines.

+ Bobby Muller—co-founder of the International Campaign to Ban Landmines, which is the co-recipient of the 1997 Nobel Peace Prize.

José Ramos-Horta

East Timor

Short Biography

In conferring the 1996 Nobel Peace Prize to two East Timorese peace activists, Bishop Carlos Ximenes Belo and José Ramos-Horta, the Nobel Committee sent a fundamental message to the world: the value and importance of respect for human rights are not measured by the numerical or political strength of an oppressed people.

East Timor forms part of one of the easternmost islands of the Indonesian archipelago. Located three hundred miles north of Australia and some nine hundred miles east of Jakarta, this tiny territory was the victim of Indonesian aggression, as well as general international acquiescence to the blatant violations of human rights and international law that were perpetrated by the Indonesian government since it invaded East Timor in 1975. In the years following that invasion, an estimated 230,000 East Timorese (one-third of an original population of 690,000) lost their lives due to starvation, epidemics, war, and terror. Economic and strategic ties to the Indonesian government led most of the world's major powers to cooperate with Jakarta without regard to the serious legal and human rights issues raised by the situation in East Timor.

East Timor was first settled by Portuguese traders in 1520. The Dutch began to expand to the island of Timor and wrested control over West Timor from the Portuguese in the seventeenth century. An 1859 treaty established the current borders. West Timor, administered as part of the Dutch East Indies, became part of Indonesia in 1946, while East Timor, with a different language, religion, and customs from its island neighbor, remained part of the Portuguese colonial empire. Unlike Indonesia, which is the most populous Muslim nation in the world, with more than 190 million people, East Timor is populated primarily by Roman Catholics.

Following the 1974 collapse of the Portuguese colonial system, the Portuguese withdrew from East Timor while retaining sovereignty over the former colony. Two political parties then vied for power, the leftist Fretilin party and the conservative Timorese Democratic Union (UDT). An initial alliance between the two parties dissolved in May 1975, and in August 1975 the UDT launched a coup. Within three weeks, the Fretilin forces completely defeated those of the UDT, and for a period of about three months, the Fretilin party controlled an independent East Timorese government. The foreign minister and United Nations representative for the fledgling government was the twenty-five-year-old José Ramos-Horta.

Two days after a December 5, 1975, state visit in Jakarta with President Suharto in which President Ford and Secretary of State Henry Kissinger pledged U.S. support and military aid, Indonesia invaded East Timor. The Indonesian government formally annexed East Timor in July 1976 as the twenty-seventh Indonesian province.

The United Nations never recognized Indonesia's sovereignty over East Timor, in part because the annexation violated the Indonesian national constitution. In its independence settlement with its former Dutch colonial masters, Indonesia renounced any claims to territories not controlled in 1942 by the Netherlands-Indies government. Despite the important principles at stake—

the right of self-determination, the sanctity of international borders, and the authority of the U.N. Security Council—international reaction to the Indonesian invasion was muted or non-existent.

Born in 1949 in Dili, the capital of East Timor, José Ramos-Horta came by his activism naturally. His father, a native of Portugal, had been deported to East Timor by the Portuguese government for protesting its military dictatorship.

In 1970, José Ramos-Horta was exiled for two years to Mozambique by the Portuguese government for his outspoken advocacy of East Timorese independence. In 1975, he fled the country only days before the Indonesian invasion. In the years since, he became the principal spokesman for his country's cause, pleading its case before the United Nations, the European Parliament, and other diplomatic and political bodies.

In his award presentation speech, Francis Sejersted, chairman of the Norwegian Nobel Committee, noted that since the invasion, Ramos-Horta has lived abroad, "unceasingly and with great personal sacrifice collecting and communicating information on the repression, torture, and killing in his home country, and acting as East Timor's principal international spokesman. At the same time, he has successfully kept up his efforts to unite the various East Timorese groups in a single national front, while constantly seeking opportunities for a peaceful solution to the conflict with Indonesia, based on respect for the integrity of the East Timorese people."

He praised both Ramos-Horta and Bishop Carlos Ximenes Belo for their "work towards a just and peaceful solution to the conflict in East Timor" and for their "sustained and self-sacrificing contributions for a small but oppressed people." On behalf of the Nobel Committee, he added his hopes that the award would "spur efforts to find a diplomatic solution to the conflict in East Timor based on the people's right to self-determination."

In 1992, Ramos-Horta began calling for a three-phase peace plan for East Timor, similar to the Israeli-Palestinian agreement.

The plan was to start with demilitarization and self-rule, and lead to a referendum and a final decision on the territory in five to ten years. He also called for the release of political prisoners, including Xanana Gusmao, the Fretilin resistance leader, captured by Indonesian troops in 1992 and sentenced to twenty years in prison.

The awarding of the Nobel Prize to Belos and Ramos-Horta served to redirect international attention to the conflict in East Timor. In May 1998, President Suharto resigned following massive protests and was replaced by former Prime Minister B.J. Habibie. On June 10, 1998, Habibie proposed a plan of limited autonomy for East Timor, linked to international recognition of Indonesian sovereignty over the territory. In 1999 full independence was gained after a referendum.

JOSÉ RAMOS-HORTA
"Democracy and Diplomacy in the Asia-Pacific Region"

First, I would like to thank so much the organizers of this conference for your kindness in inviting me and giving a platform to the often voiceless people of East Timor. I bring to you the warmest greetings of my good friend and co-laureate of the 1996 Peace Prize, Bishop Carlos Felipe Ximenes Belo.

This morning, as I was sitting next to my good friend Oscar Arias in the bus coming here, I asked him, "Do you have a written speech?" He said he does, and that's when I got nervous because if Oscar Arias, such a brilliant, wonderful statesman, brings a written speech, and I don't have a written speech—he literally spoiled my morning. So, I have to apologize to you if my speech is a rambling one.

Let me start by sharing with you a story. A few years ago, I was in Sweden, and paid a courtesy call to the Cuban Ambassador in Stockholm. A colleague accompanied me to the meeting. After the meeting, my colleague told me, "If your intention was to tell the Cuban Ambassador how the situation in East Timor was very confused, you did a very good job, because the man was totally confused. You mixed three languages throughout the discussion. Why the hell didn't you just speak in Portuguese?" So, please, my apologies if my English is not clear enough, eloquent enough, to convey to you what the people of East Timor feel, and what I feel.

To situate the question of East Timor and the region in its historical and geopolitical context—you might recall a picture that made headlines in 1975. An American helicopter was trying to land on the rooftop of the U.S. Embassy in Saigon to rescue American diplomats, CIA officials, South Vietnamese collaborators. Soon after the collapse of U.S. presence in South Vietnam, Cambodia and then Laos followed. Better than a thousand words, that picture illustrated the humiliating retreat of one of the two superpowers from a peasant war in Asia. In another continent the same year, the Portuguese empire had collapsed. Cuban/Soviet forces entered the battleground for influence in Angola. Mozambique became independent under a Marxist movement. The battle between East and West for influence in Southern Africa raged on. In the horn of Africa, Haile Selassie of Ethiopia had been overthrown, again shifting the balance of power to the Soviet side. The Soviet Union was already in control, so to speak, in Somalia—with the collapse of Haile Selassie, a Marxist regime took over. It seemed as if the "domino theory" first articulated by Lyndon Johnson, which served as a strategic rationale for U.S. intervention in China, was being confirmed.

It was against this background that then-President Gerald Ford and Secretary of State Kissinger visited Indonesia, on December 6, 1975. Within twelve hours of their departure, East Timor was invaded by Indonesia. East Timor, a country of 700,000 then, 95 percent subsistence farmers, peasants, squeezed in an area of only 19,000 square kilometers, was to experience in the following years one of the worst massacres—amounting to genocide—since the end of World War II. The tens of thousands of people who died in East Timor in the following days, weeks, months, and years were, in fact, just a footnote to the Cold War, a casualty of realpolitik and pragmatism of states. We, the East Timorese, join the Tibetans, the Kurdish, the Armenians in the past, the Palestinians, the Gypsies, and the Jews for centuries, as expendable peoples, as casualties of the grand scheme of the larger powers. Some of the Palestinians have managed to survive and get out of oblivion, at least cease to be ignored. But if we were to try to understand why all of this happened, what happened to the Jews for centuries, to the Tibetans for the past fifty years, to the Kurdish in endless wars, to the East Timorese, I would say, we are all sacrificed in the order of realpolitik and pragmatism of states.

One issue that always captured my attention—even though I come from a very remote island far away from the Middle Eastern region—I was always fascinated by one people, the Jews. As a young teenager in the sixties, I would relentlessly look for books on Jewish history. One thing I could not comprehend: the persecution, the discrimination, the killing of the Jews. Then a few years ago, I found out that apart from my Asian and African heritage, I have some Jewish heritage as well, going back to the Inquisition. Maybe that is the reason for my curiosity. But *why* were the Jews almost literally thoroughly destroyed in the thirties? What *wrong* did they do? A powerless group of people. No power behind them. It was prejudice, ignorance for centuries that led to the hatred towards the Jews. But if those who were so hateful of the Jews were to *read* and *study* their extraordinary culture—the wealth, the richness of their history and their culture, their music—maybe those years, centuries of persecution and discrimination, would not have happened.

My contention, my belief, is that it is ignorance of each other that feeds into prejudice. Prejudice leads to suspicion and then conflict. I do not wish to oversimplify; there are other reasons for wars, such as fighting to control natural resources, territory, but a lot of the wars in the past and today are caused by prejudices because of ignorance, and then mistrust and fear of the other side. We, the East Timorese, join all these peoples—the Jews, the Palestinians, the Tibetans, the Burmese, the Armenians in the past— in this long list of endless conflict, people sacrificed in all the pragmatism and realpolitik.

Twenty-three years ago, no one thought the East Timorese could survive the onslaught. Every major country in the world provided weapons to Indonesia; countries that preach democracy and human rights were the ones that provided the most weapons not only to Indonesia but to many dictators around the world. All kinds of weapons were unleashed on the people of East Timor. Twenty-three years later, we are there kicking, surviving, and it is the Indonesian empire that is collapsing around us. The Suharto dictatorship is gone. There is a dynamic, lively democracy movement taking shape in Indonesia, and Indonesian people are beginning to ask, What have we done to this small nation of East Timor? Who is going to explain to the Indonesians the loss of their own people—that thousands of Indonesian soldiers, young people, lost their lives in the fields of East Timor? Who is going to explain to the Indonesian people the hundreds of millions of dollars wasted in weapons purchases instead of channeling them to education, health care, clean water, housing for their people?

The West has something to answer as well. With the end of the Cold War, we thought there would be less conflict, but, since the end of the Cold War, as Europe could no longer find much of a market in Europe itself for their weapons, they actively promote weapon sales to the poorest countries of the south. We became the market, the dumping ground, for the excess weapons produced by the democracies of the north. I will not elaborate much on this topic because our good friend Oscar will address this issue. But the collapse of the East Asian myth—of the East Asian tiger economies—Malaysia, Indonesia, Thailand, South Korea—as painful as these economic collapses are for the millions of people in the region, opened extraordinary opportunities for democracy and the rule of law to finally triumph and prevail in the region. Those events have destroyed the so-called Asian values that have been advanced for many years by Mahathir Mohamad of Malaysia, Lee Kuan Yew of Singapore, Li Peng of China, and Suharto of Indonesia—Asian values that are supposedly unique and stand against the Universal Declaration of Human Rights, which is supposed to be, according to them, a Western concept. Millions of people pouring into the streets of Rangoon, Bangkok, Manila, Indonesia, and South Korea are telling their leaders that human rights, democracy, rule of law are also *our* aspirations, are also *our* rights. That is the extraordinary opportunity offered by this economic and financial collapse in the region.

As I speak here today, I must say thanks, President Clinton, for the U.S. leadership in this current crisis in the region. Sometimes I think back on the criticism that people addressed at the U.S., but the reality is when the need comes, it has been the U.S., and particularly this administration, that has offered the necessary leadership for economic recovery in East Asia, for peace in the Middle East, in Bosnia, Kosovo, and Northern Ireland. Again it was Clinton, after many, many years of Africa being ignored, being off the agenda, being off the radar screen of the U.S. administration, who put Africa back on the map. I say, "Thank you, Mr. President." And thank you for the modest things you are doing on East Timor. I hope that in the last two years of his administration, he will forcefully support the emerging democracy in Indonesia, support the economic recovery, and use his abilities, his extraordinary energy and creativity, to finally bring about peace in East Timor.

Lastly, let me share with you a story. A few years ago, I was driving from Lausanne, Switzerland to Geneva to attend yet one more of those almost futile exercises at the U.N. Commission on Human Rights. I tuned in to the BBC, the only good thing the British ever invented—I know it is a wild exaggeration, and my sincere apologies to any British subject in the room, but it is my favorite radio station, the best anywhere in the world. Tuning in to the BBC at eight in the morning, I heard this extraordinary news of a Soviet cosmonaut who had gone into space a few months earlier when the Soviet Union was the Soviet Union: as he prepared his spacecraft to return to earth, the startling news came from Moscow, "Do not come back. Your country no longer exists." Just imagine someone out of Houston, Texas telling John Glenn, "Don't come back." If it had been certain other U.S. politicians, I would like to hear someone telling them not to come back, but John Glenn, please come back. The Soviet Union had ceased to exist—the mighty empire had ceased to exist. Someone, offering a second thought from Moscow, told him, "Circle the earth a few more times," and he diligently did. In Moscow, it was disarray; no one knew what to do with him. Finally, after many hours, they brought him back to earth. The empire had ceased to exist; Armenia became independent; the Baltic States were liberated; Vaclav Havel became president of the new Republic of Czechoslovakia, now the Czech Republic; Poland and all the other countries in Eastern Europe, Central Europe, became independent, contradicting those who have told us year after year that we must accept the irreversibility of military occupations, the rule of force. The East Timorese, Tibetans, Burmese, and Kurdish remember this extraordinary lesson; we will survive. We will win.

Thank you.

Discussion Among the Participants

Julian Bond: Earlier this summer, there seemed to be some movement toward discussions of extending democracy, but lately, not much. And secondarily, what role does Portugal play?

José Ramos-Horta: I will start with the last point. Portugal has had a remarkable attitude in support of the struggle for East Timor. Having colonized East Timor for five hundred years, they woke up to their responsibilities, and, in spite of the fact that it is one of the poorest countries in Europe, they have put up a valiant effort in support of East Timor. The Secretary-General Kofi Annan— the best Secretary-General the U.N. has had in at least thirty years—has also put enormous effort in this issue, bringing Portugal, Indonesia, and myself to the negotiating table. There is a genuine move in Indonesia towards resolving this issue, in spite of their extraordinary problems; they realize it is one of the most costly problems to them. But, as in a situation of transition, like anyplace, there is lack of cohesiveness, lack of direction, lack of a central authority to make the necessary move. Thus, we have to wait a few more months for clarification in Indonesia. Right now, we are discussing an autonomy plan presented by the U.N., drafted by a professor at the Fletcher School of Law and Diplomacy, and it really is a good, good plan. If Indonesia agrees to it, with minor changes as is normal in negotiations, we could have in place by next year the implementation of this autonomy plan, leading in two, three, or five years to a referendum to determine the final status of the territory. [A referendum was conducted in August, 1999, in which the East Timorese overwhelmingly called for independence.]

And I must report that when my good friend Oscar Arias and I spoke on the phone a few weeks ago, I asked him to be the leader of advisors to the East Timorese negotiating team, and he agreed. When I informed my colleagues, they were all thrilled that Oscar

Arias had accepted to be our advisor—someone who brought about peace in Central America when the two superpowers were fighting each other in Central America. That's why I thought, If he can pull that off in Central America, he can help us in East Timor.

Jody Williams: I have a question, not specific to Indonesia and East Timor. You were talking about ignorance and prejudice being causes of conflict. The reason I ask this question is that we are contemplating how to resolve conflict hopefully before it happens, and thus at this time when there is great emphasis on the new millennium, how we can teach the world to do things differently. Is ignorance and prejudice the cause, or, as we saw in Rwanda and other places, are those fighting for power and exploiting the ignorance the cause? It may seem like a semantic difference, but I think it's important, because it helps us decide how we go about preventing conflict. If it is the powers that be that are fighting for power—and using everything at their disposal, including arms of war, including ignorance, including prejudice—then we have to attack the problem from many different angles. So this is the question I ask: "How do we attack the problem—from the top down, from the bottom up, from all sides?"

José Ramos-Horta: Yes, certainly, I did not mean to attribute to ignorance, prejudice, that it is the sole reason. There are others, such as often a nation's quest for survival in terms of even water resources, mineral resources, and so on. You are absolutely right. In Bosnia and in Rwanda, for instance, a few individuals in their quest for power irresponsibly ignited prejudices and hatred by instilling fears in a given group. How to solve it? I tell you, I don't have a clue. The only thing I could say is that yes, diplomatic intervention and mediation are obviously necessary, like you have in Bosnia. There has been a lot of criticism of the Bosnia Peace Accord, but Richard Holbrooke did outstanding work in Bosnia, as he has done in Kosovo, and so on, because at least guns fall silent.

But this does not address the root of our problem. I still believe that in the long run, beyond the band-aid type of diplomacy which is peacemaking and signing treaties, you need to go for community dialogue. I was surprised in Greece recently when I asked a Greek journalist whether, in the case of Cyprus, there is much ongoing dialogue between the Greek Cypriots and Turkish Cypriots. He said, "Yes, there is some, but not much." Between the position of the Greek authorities in Greece and the Turkish government, there is something missing, and that is the people who inhabit that island, and if there is not much dialogue going by academics, by students, by labor leaders, by NGOs, then if you let the situation go on and on, then something that probably was false, was artificial a few years earlier, becomes part of the history, part of the culture. The process of dialogue leads towards reconciliation; education leads towards peace, but it takes a long, long time. It does not produce a result like in a peace treaty—signed between two parties as you have done in Bosnia and Kosovo, with the threat of force behind it. Dialogue is the only way, I think.

In our case, in East Timor in the last several months, since January, 1998, we have been making repeated appeals to our people on the ground: "Please, we don't want to see one single Indonesian migrant touched; we don't want to see one single house burned." With the collapse of the regime and because we have so many migrants in Timor, the temptation to exact revenge on them is great. So even before the collapse of Suharto back in January, we began a massive, active campaign of telling our people not to use violence on innocent migrants. And so far, beyond some occasional verbal abuse, not one single Indonesian migrant has been harmed, and not one single house has been torched. But this process will take months and years.

Harn Yawnghwe: I know it might be a sensitive topic, but I was wondering if you could elaborate on this: Although President

Habibie is initiating dialogue with East Timor, I know that in Indonesia there are some people who fear that if East Timor is given autonomy, it might lead other islands within the Indonesian nation to ask for more autonomy. Are there people who might be in opposition to autonomy for this reason?

José Ramos-Horta: Yes, there is genuine fear—unfounded, but genuine fear—on the part of some Indonesians because Indonesia is a huge archipelago of thousands of islands, 250 to 300 ethnic groups speaking 500 languages, and they fear that letting go East Timor will set a precedent. The ex-Soviet Union and ex-Yugoslavia scenarios are not very good inducements to them to let go of Timor. But the fact of the matter is that East Timor was never part of Indonesia. East Timor is predominantly Catholic, 95 percent. It was colonized by Portugal for almost five hundred years. Culturally, ethnically, historically, it is different; so, it does not fit into the Indonesian historical boundaries. Whether those fears are founded or not, the reality is that there are some people who fear granting autonomy to East Timor. But, at the same time, we say: the longer you stay on in East Timor, the more costly it is for you, and that is when it could cause the unraveling of the Indonesian Republic. I, personally, do not believe that Indonesia could disintegrate just because East Timor becomes independent. It doesn't work like that. You have to have real movement on the ground in Indonesia, of people wanting to separate from Indonesia for this to happen. And, so far, although there are some protests in other parts of Indonesia, by and large it's not over the question of independence or sovereignty—they just want more autonomy to deal with their cultural and economic matters. East Timor, therefore, is unique in this regard.

Increasingly, there are many, many people in Indonesia, including very important Muslim leaders such as Dr. Amien Rais, who are calling for a referendum on self-determination in East

Timor. There are people at the top of the military who are also calling for a referendum in East Timor. So I believe if we, on our side, are also responsible enough to be flexible and creative to enable the Indonesians to get disengaged from East Timor gradually, without loss of face, with honor, with dignity, and if we look into a long-term strategy, not seeking independence a year from now, or two years from now, who knows? In five, ten years from now, the new Indonesia would see an independent East Timor as very normal. That's our belief, and that is the strategy we are pursuing.

Julian Bond: Your co-recipient, Bishop Belo, has been engaging in some talks. How are these progressing?

José Ramos-Horta: Bishop Belo is a remarkable, extraordinary individual. He is in Timor, and he has been, particularly in the last few months, busy engaging East Timorese society itself in approaches of reconciliation. A bit like in South Africa and other places torn by conflict, there are divisions within our own community—people who have collaborated with the occupation and tremendous resentment towards those who collaborated. And so, we all are engaged in this process of dialogue, reconciliation, because although there is an ample opportunity now, a golden opportunity, to resolve the problem of East Timor, if we don't, at the same time, embark on a process of reconciliation, we could lose this opportunity—if the East Timorese begin to fight each other over the past twenty-three years of collaboration with the Indonesian army. A lot of people collaborated for different reasons—for fear, for money—and we view our collaborators largely as victims of the whole war itself. I do not think that, in our case, a society, a country, can heal itself if soon after victory you embark on persecuting those who were on the other side.

But at the same time, you are confronted with a dilemma. Look at the case of Chile—what to do with Pinochet? Personally, I am, of course, on the side of the victims of the Pinochet regime, but if

I were to confront an eighty-two-year-old man who has only two or three years more of life, and have to make a decision: put him on trial, in prison, or send him back home, I probably would be tempted to go to the softer side. I was in Chile a year ago, and whenever I talked to the victims of Pinochet—victims of torture, women who were raped—I was angry. Angry that the culprits were still there. But then when I see this old man, on the verge of going to jail, I say, "Probably best to just send him home." I am not very good at dispensing justice, as you can see.

Julian Bond: I think some of us in the United States look on the South African experience with envy that we did not, at a time in our country, begin such a process, and perhaps it is not too late. But how can you in East Timor embark on this process of reconciliation even before you've achieved your goal of autonomy? Is it possible to begin now?

José Ramos-Horta: Yes, it is possible for two reasons. One, a pragmatic reason on our part, is that we must extend a hand to every Timorese, in order to reduce the field of maneuver of our adversary. The fewer people on the other side, the better. So, I'm not saying that our strategy is purely altruistic, purely moral. It is also political. Also, although the country is small, so many people have died already, and I tell you, frankly, no one is clean in this conflict in East Timor. We, the East Timorese, fought each other too in 1975, and many people were killed unnecessarily. Indonesia invaded East Timor; it shouldn't have done so—no reason whatsoever for a country invading another. But, at the same time, looking back, it was 1975, post-Vietnam, Cold War; maybe we understand Indonesia's fears at the time—that an independent East Timor could turn into another Cuba. That was the argument at the time. Rightly or wrongly, that is their fear. And the post-Vietnam U.S., having just come out of Indochina—I also understand, why would they bother about East Timor? So, they turned the other way around and allowed Indonesia to resolve a potential Communist problem. The reality is that, in the end, we were the ones who were victims, remain victims today, and I just hope that we all seize on this opportunity to redress the wrongs done to the people of East Timor. First, yes, we have to be courageous enough and humble enough—courage and humility go hand-in-hand—to say, "Well, it is not only Indonesia that is at fault, not only the U.S., or Australia." First we, the East Timorese, must ask ourselves and address our responsibility in this conflict.

Julian Bond: Mr. President, let me turn to you, in your role as adviser. What are you going to suggest be done that is not being done?

President Oscar Arias Sánchez: It seems to me that the international community should support the East Timorese, and what you need is political will. The U.N. has taken this issue, and Kofi Annan is very determined, committed, and supportive. Negotiations need patience, humility, political will, and the knowledge that you need to compromise. Certainly, the Indonesians should understand and should know that the international community is with the East Timorese. There is not much I could add, but they deserve to become an independent nation, and the international community should support them in this task.

Questions from the Audience

Jeffrey Hopkins: There are a great many questions from the audience. This one is to all of the laureates, but perhaps we could address it to Bobby Muller. What led you to believe that you could make a change?

Bobby Muller: It was the most natural thing for me to believe, honestly. You know, I had come down to Washington in 1978, as I was an angry Vietnam veteran. I had served in Vietnam as a marine infantry officer, took a bullet through the chest, wound up paralyzed from the chest down, came back and spent a year in a veterans' hospital. My hospital was the cover story of *Life Magazine* in the second largest selling issue that *Life Magazine* had ever put out, because it represented the deplorable conditions. Despite the pictures of the overcrowding and the dilapidated facilities, that article could never convey the stench of that hospital, or the despair that permeated it. The fact that eight of my friends, including my closest friend, committed suicide is perhaps better testimony to those conditions. I figured that, having been a marine officer and spending literally hundreds of thousands of dollars a day to kill people, day after day, it was simply a matter of informing the American people about what was going on with its veterans—at least in some cases, as in mine—and that justice would be realized.

So I went to law school and I got a law degree, but I realized that one of the very few places within our system of law that you don't have the right to go to court is to petition any grievances against the Veterans' Administration. So, I said, well that's not going to work—maybe we need some new laws, and maybe we need some advocacy. And as one angry guy, I went to Washington and I started to talk. The second week I was there, the editor of *The Washington Post* editorial page called, "Hey, I heard you talk, I like what you have to say; come on in and let's talk a little more." He wound up giving me and the effort that we put together about thirty-five editorials in one year in *The Washington Post* and on the op-ed page. *The New York Times* picked it up, and when *The New York Times* picks you up, you wind up being on network television. So I did "Good Morning America" five times, did the "Phil Donahue Show" seven times, and basically, got a message out there. The end result was we created a national organization, getting a Congressional Charter in 1986. It took a bunch of years, but we got it. We set up programs for Vet Centers, and we set up agent orange programs.

The long and the short is that, in this country, the truth is that we are a democracy. We actually have the machinery to exercise that democracy. It's a little rusty; a lot of us have lost faith and confidence in the fact that you can really engage the gears and make it happen, but I had the good fortune of seeing a real success. So, in the work that I was doing—in going back to Indochina and seeing the travesty that was played out in Cambodia, particularly with landmines—and coming to understand what was going on, I concluded that with knowledge comes responsibility. When you know about a situation that obviously 99 percent of Americans had not a clue about, there's a little bit of an obligation to carry that message home. When you realize how devastating landmines are, you really have no doubt but that with an educated populace, landmines will go on the same list as poison gas after World War I, biological weapons, and chemical weapons, etc., about which the world community says, "Yes, these mechanisms might kill people, but the overall costs of putting them into play are too prohibitive, and we're going to outlaw them." Honest to God, as strange as it may seem—I had absolutely no doubt but that we would get there, and get this weapon effectively banned. The only question we had was how much time it was going to take.

Jeffrey Hopkins: Perhaps the next question we should address to Dr. Menchú Tum. What has sustained you in your long fight?

Dr. Rigoberta Menchú Tum: I am sorry. I don't speak English [text follows through an interpreter, as do all of Dr. Menchú Tum's remarks during the conference]. I believe when one becomes involved in a struggle, it is a daily struggle; it is not an occasional struggle—it is not to take advantage of a particular situation. In my case, my focus comes from the fact that I was born Maya, and when people ask me about indigenous groups in the world, I am profoundly partial. Guatemala lived through one of the bloodiest wars in Central America. Thus far, we have been able to document 424 townships destroyed during the armed conflict. In this situation, unfortunately, I lost my parents, I lost many friends; I knew many people who struggled for justice, and they never got to see the end of the war. That's why I think peace is not the product of one person; it is in the first place the conviction of all the parties involved in the conflict. The building of peace is carried out by the people themselves—it is of the *pueblo,* of the women, of the children—not by the Nobel Laureates. We Nobel Laureates are an elite, a privileged group that can push forward some processes, but the social actor is the most important, and I consider myself a social actor.

Jeffrey Hopkins: This is a question I think we should address to Archbishop Tutu. What impact did receiving the Nobel Peace Prize have on your ability to move toward your goals?

Archbishop Desmond Tutu: Well, it has the effect of turning you into an oracle. Things you said before you got the Nobel Peace Prize, and not too many people paid attention—you say the same things, and people think it's pearls from Heaven!

Jeffrey Hopkins: I think we should address this question to Betty Williams. Given that this historic meeting is taking place at the University of Virginia and in Charlottesville, which is a region historically situated as the birthplace of the founding institutions of the U.S. nation, do you have any advice for our often divided ethnic and religious conflicts in contemporary U.S. culture? As an African-American woman, I worry about how we resolve U.S. conflicts within, but we need help from the outside.

Betty Williams: That's a *huge* question. There is great injustice in the United States. Anybody who denies that is blind or lying. When racism was more out front, you knew the enemy; it's more insidious now. I agree that outside help is necessary. Perhaps I agree because I live now in the United States of America and I am one who loves this country, but I also see the problems here. I mean, how dare we call a society democratic that has twelve million hungry children! There is no democracy where there is that kind of hunger.

I sometimes get terribly confused, even within myself, because I have trouble with my own bigotries. When I am really pushed into a corner, the Catholic in me stands up. I totally understand how the African-American woman who wrote that question must feel. I think peace begins with me; it is the individual that makes the difference. Whoever wrote that question, you have the power within yourself to change what is wrong in your society.

Jeffrey Hopkins: I'll address the next question to Jody Williams. If ignorance is a key factor in the lack of peace, do you think that the Internet's ability to share information quickly and universally will help us achieve peace?

Jody Williams: There is tremendous mythology about the role of the Internet in the Landmine Campaign. What was important in the Landmine Campaign, apart from many other things, was the desire to involve a huge array of groups and individuals immediately. We did that from the beginning through fax machines. When you are trying to bring together lots of people who have huge agendas of their own in their own organizations, they need to believe that their immediate input in the growth of whatever you're doing is important. So we used the fax initially. But it is also more than that. It's the individual. It's sharing information, but it's making people believe they are part of the process. Not just information. Information by itself can be overwhelming. We got to the point with the speedy use of e-mail where colleagues in the campaign would say to me, "Stop sending so much information— why don't you just send a summary?" You can have too much information. I agree with Betty absolutely, completely, about individual responsibility, to want to make change, to take whatever the information is and decide how to use it to contribute to a process of change. Information, by itself, can't do anything. It's how you use it.

One other point I've worried about of late, is governments seeking to restrict communication on the Internet. Recently I was in Spain where there was a meeting of police from around the world to deal with terrorism. They were citing Mr. Bin Laden and his use of the Internet to set up his terrorist activities. That may or may not be true, but what I worried about immediately was that the powers that be were going to use that kind of example, which may or may not be true, to try to crush actual, legitimate use of the information highway. I noticed the same thing with the uprising in Chiapas. The combatants in Chiapas were able immediately to use the information highway to get their information out, and politicians immediately responded, "This is inappropriate, this is terrorism on the Internet." I worry that there will be a backlash and an attempt to stifle information. I think it is very complicated, much more so than people seem to realize.

Betty Williams

Northern Ireland

Short Biography

Sometimes a Nobel Peace Laureate is created in an instant. Such is the case with Betty Williams, a native of Belfast, Ireland, whose intuitive, immediate response to a senseless act of violence created the Northern Ireland Peace Movement.

Having grown up in Belfast, Williams—the first child of a Catholic mother and Protestant father—was sickened by the increasing violence in her community. In 1973, a British soldier was shot before her eyes, but even that horror did not prepare her for the event she would witness three years later.

On August 10, 1976, a getaway car bearing an IRA gunman lost control when its driver was fatally shot by pursuing British soldiers. The careening car slammed into Anne Maguire and her three young children who were out for a stroll in the sunshine. Williams, who lived in the neighborhood where the incident took place, heard the sound of the car smashing into an iron fence alongside where the Maguires had been walking and ran to investigate. First on the scene, she was appalled by what she saw—two children dead, a third mortally wounded, and the mother critically injured.

Herself a mother of two, the thirty-four-year-old Williams was overwhelmed by a passionate desire to take a stand against the violence that precipitated nightmares like the one before her. As soon as she could leave the accident site, she acted on her instincts and began canvassing her neighbors. Within two days she had collected six thousand signatures on a petition that demanded peace and a stop to the violence. Despite fear of reprisals against her by Ireland's warring factions, she appeared in a local television broadcast and appealed to Ireland's women—both Catholic and Protestant—to work with her to rid their community of "this riffraff."

Her appeal generated a response from many people, including Mairead Maguire, Anne Maguire's sister and aunt to the three slain children. Together, Williams and Maguire organized a peace march of ten thousand Protestant and Catholic women. The marchers were physically assaulted by members of the Irish Republican Army, a violent pro-independence group, who called them dupes of the British. Nonetheless, they succeeded in their trek to the gravesites of the Maguire children. A week later, thirty-five thousand Belfasters marched for peace from a Catholic area of the city to a Protestant area—again led by Williams and Maguire.

Newspaper reporter Ciaran McKeown joined the women's efforts. They embraced his suggestion to form an organization called the Community of Peace People, which had a dual mission to help end sectarian fighting in Northern Ireland and to provide services for victims of the area's violence. The resulting peace movement attracted worldwide publicity.

Few would have thought a peace movement possible, especially in such a short amount of time. Ever since England's King Henry VIII (1509-1547) sent Protestants to colonize Ireland and wrest control away from the country's Gaelic and Roman Catholic native population, Williams' homeland had been plagued by violence. Through the centuries, Irish Catholics had staged numerous rebellions to regain their country's independence from Britain, while Irish Protestants, loyal to the British union, had steadfastly countered to maintain English control.

Following World War I, pro-independence guerrilla groups, such as the IRA, wore down British resolve. In 1922, England established by treaty the Irish Free State, a twenty-six-county area in the south of Ireland whose population is predominately Catholic. Excluded from this treaty were six counties in Northern Ireland, which contained a Protestant majority. While the treaty was a step in the direction of Irish independence, it gave England continuing control over a large area of the country indefinitely. The IRA and Sinn Fein, another pro-independence organization, repudiated the treaty.

Fifteen years after its creation, the Irish Free State revised its constitution to remove all references to British sovereignty, asserting its jurisdiction over all thirty-two counties on the island. In 1949, it became the Republic of Ireland, and in the decades to follow, the IRA campaign for a unified Ireland intensified. In the late 1960s Britain sent military troops to Northern Ireland to act as a police force, but the action only escalated the violence between the IRA and groups loyal to Britain.

As the capital of Northern Ireland, Belfast was a frequent target for unbridled IRA bombings and murders—primarily against British soldiers, but also against Protestant and Catholic civilians. Protestant extremists formed paramilitary units such as the Ulster Freedom Fighters, which countered the IRA's violence with similar acts of their own.

It was against this backdrop of spiraling violence that Betty Williams said "enough." For her efforts in trying to bring peace to Northern Ireland, she received the 1976 Carl von Ossietsky Medal for Courage from the Berlin section of the International League of Human Rights. Williams was also jointly honored with Maguire as a recipient of the 1976 Nobel Peace Prize for their grassroots work that spawned the Northern Ireland Peace Movement. In presenting the prize to Williams and Maguire, Norwegian Nobel Committee vice-chairman Egil Aarvik said, "One of the reasons why the women proved so successful in their campaign is that on both sides of the frontline, a desperate yearning for peace had taken root. What Betty Williams and Mairead Maguire said reechoed the thoughts of tens of thousands, and in this way they became the spokesmen of the desire for a common-sense approach that filled the average man and woman—despite their feeling of helplessness in the face of violence."

In 1978 Williams and Maguire stepped down from their leadership roles in the Peace People. Eventually Williams emigrated to the United States. In the twenty-two years since receiving the Nobel Peace Prize, she has traveled around the world, lecturing on peace and working with fellow laureates to advance the cause of peace.

Williams has received numerous honors since receiving the Nobel Peace Prize, such as an honorary Doctor of Law degree from Yale University, the Schweitzer Medallion for Courage, the Martin Luther King Jr. Award, and the Eleanor Roosevelt Award. In 1992, Texas Governor Ann Richards appointed Williams to the Texas Commission for Children and Youth.

Acting on her special interest in promoting the safety and well-being of children, Williams founded the World Centers of Compassion for Children (WCCC) in 1997. A non-profit organization headquartered in Gulf Breeze, Florida, the organization is dedicated to creating "safe and nurturing environments" for children in areas devastated by war, conflict, and poverty. Williams serves as president of WCCC. She is also chair of the Institute for Asian Democracy in Washington, D.C., and was named a member of the International Honorary Committee for the twenty-fifth anniversary of the Children's Defense Fund.

BETTY WILLIAMS
"Children's Rights:
The Need to Establish Safe Havens for Children of War"

Good morning, everybody. [*Audience responds, "Good Morning."*]
Good! You're alive! Let's do it again. Good Morning! [*Audience
responds louder, "Good Morning!"*] That makes me feel a little better. It might not make you feel any better, but it makes me feel
better. I'm always terribly nervous when I get up to speak because
before I became a Nobel Laureate, I only ever spoke in public
once before in my life, which was at my sister's wedding when my
Daddy got a little tiddly and I had to stand up and thank all the
guests. And Father Tutu was not a great help. He said coming out,
"Are you going to perform?" I'm not quite sure what that means.
I just know that within me there is an incredible passion to change
the world for the children. Bobby said earlier that he started his
work because he was angry. I guess that's why mine started. People
say to me, "Why did you start the Movement for Peace in Northern Ireland?" The truth is I did it for purely selfish reasons. Their
names are Deborah and Paul, my children. I didn't want my ba-
bies to be brought up in a society that was destroying children.

And so, the Movement for Peace in Northern Ireland was begun by women. I believe that women have a huge role to play in
creating a just, non-violent, and peaceful world. Now, that doesn't
mean that we ostracize men. Ladies, get real. We cannot do it
without our partners walking beside us. During the last political
campaign in the United States of America, for President Clinton,
the catch phrase then was, "It's the economy, stupid." To the men
of the world I say, "It's a *womb* thing, stupid." Stop taking my
children. Stop destroying my creation. Many years ago, we opened
a school in Northern Ireland, the first integrated school in Northern Ireland's history, called Lagan College. When we opened the

school, we asked the children would they name the school—now there's a great fondness in Ireland for saints, it's St. Dominic, St. Patrick, St. Theresa, Saint, Saint, Saint, Saint. So we asked the children to name the school. And, out of the mouths of babes and sucklings come the most incredible words. One little boy, about ten years old, said, "Why do we have to call everything here after saints? There's a river in the middle of Belfast, it's called Lagan, the Lagan River. Why can't we call it Lagan College?" Then we asked the children to design the motto of the school; they designed a bridge over the river, with two little hands going across that bridge. Perhaps it's time that we, as adults, give more credibility to what comes out of the mouths of babes and sucklings.

Changing the world for the children. My goodness, what a huge statement to make. If you look at the world as it is now, you will see that we are in an economic crisis. I mean, a person with half a brain knows that there is an economic crisis going on in the world. Every time there is an injustice of that kind, economically, socially, or culturally, it always falls to the littlest of our citizens to do the most suffering. You see the way I said "citizens"? Because they *are* citizens. When our work was born in Northern Ireland, it was born because I saw three little citizens destroyed in one huge act of senseless, useless violence.

I often say to people, "Tears without action are wasted sentiment." You can cry all the tears that you want to, and that's not going to change anything. The women of Northern Ireland stood up and said they'd had enough—that was twenty-three years ago— what you see today evolving is not that Gerry Adams finished the war in Northern Ireland. That's a lie. Gerry didn't finish the war in Northern Ireland. There was a groundswell that became so strong and so huge in its justice that, really, the men of violence had nowhere else to go. They had to get around a table. They had to begin discussing. Father Tutu has just returned from Northern

Ireland, and he said to me, "You know, Trimble has never shaken the hand of Gerry Adams." Well, I'll tell you something: Gerry Adams wouldn't be the first terrorist who became a statesman, would he? Someday, they will shake hands.

My work was born because of an act of violence. You see, there are no famous people in the world, ladies and gentlemen; there are only people who *think* they are. Who would want to hear what Betty Williams, ordinary housewife—did you ever here such a disgusting word as an "ordinary housewife"? Have you ever met an *ordinary* housewife? Have ya? Hands up. See, there's no such thing as ordinary in the world. Everybody is extraordinary. And everybody can do something. Little did I know when I stood up that morning and screamed out against the violence, what God's plan was—because you know, God has a very strange sense of humor. You never see a sentence as it's written, you only see it when the whole paragraph is completed. So, He stuck this Nobel label on me and threw me out in the world. I very quickly became an expert in the issues of children.

One of the first journeys—I would prefer to tell you the stories that children tell me, rather than talk as Betty Williams. Talk as the children talk to me. One of the first journeys that I took was to Ethiopia. We went in with convoys of trucks delivering food around the little villages. When you go to an area like that, it doesn't take too long before you start to suffer from what the people there are forced to live with on a daily basis. You get head lice—anywhere you have hair you have lice, which is very uncomfortable. You also get a terribly sick stomach, and then, after three or four days when you start to try to acclimatize, you become kind of emaciated. We covered about thirty-two villages in that journey. They were all absolutely horrible, but I'll just tell you about the last village that we visited. By then, we were almost out of supplies, and we were all very tired. We were also emotionally destroyed. This village had 368 children. Let me rephrase that: 368 little pieces of human garbage, because that's what we had made of these children. In a world that can feed itself, it's crazy that any child should starve. And we didn't know what to do for these children because we were so destroyed emotionally at the time. But I managed to get friendly with an Ethiopian guard. I really kissed the Blarney Stone that morning, Father Tutu, because I actually had to physically say to myself, "Don't hate this person, don't hate this person," because he was one of the people who would be responsible for terrible actions. But I managed to get friendly with him, and he let me use his telephone equipment. I called a friend of mine in Norway, a wonderful man called Gunnar Borrevik, who was head of a newspaper called *Faedrelandsvennen,* which is rather on a par with *The New York Times;* they flew in a small aircraft, and we started transporting children to a field hospital the Norwegians had set up. It would have taken us probably about five days by road to get the children to the field hospital, but it only took twenty minutes by air. This was only a little six-seater plane, and into it we put forty children. On a journey of twenty minutes, we lost fourteen of those children. Fourteen children. Think about that. Those priorities—they talk to me about military budgets; I have to sit in rooms with men who justify military budgets by telling me it's for defense. Do you know what I say? "No doubt, the dead and dying are very gratified that you are defending them so well." The insanity of what's going on militarily in the world has got to be challenged. Not by me, or Jody Williams, or His Holiness, or anybody else who is supposed to have "a famous name." The insanity of that has got to be challenged by every single one of you. Every one of you. I'm proud to have a friend by the name of Oscar Arias Sánchez, because this man is challenging that, and we must all support that challenge. To look forward to a demilitarized world is not for idealistic fools.

They call us idealistic fools—I've been referred to by many names, but that's one I object to the most. It's not idealistic to say that the world must begin to live together without guns or bombs, or better and bigger ways to destroy each other. It's not idealistic.

After having done twenty-three years of journeying around the world on behalf of children, I've come to one conclusion, and one conclusion only. The children must be given their own voice, because the adults are not doing a very good job of representing them. So, what we will do at World Centers of Compassion for Children is to create a political voice, to create a strong voice. The AARP was founded by a woman who, one day in her kitchen, was absolutely disgusted by what was happening to the elderly folk in the United States of America. She formed an organization called the American Association of Retired Persons. Everybody in Washington laughed; they thought it was a joke. The organization began to call itself "The Gray Panthers." Well, they ain't laughing anymore in Washington at those little old ladies, because when they go to Washington with an agenda, they have a voice. We will do the same for the children.

We will have to develop courts that deal with their issues separately, because the children of the world need a Marshall Plan, a huge new plan. UNESCO is wonderful, UNICEF is wonderful, Save the Children is wonderful, and on, and on, and on. But all these organizations that are out there have one problem—nobody knows what the other one's doing, and they're all fighting about their dollars. That's got to stop. We must umbrella every organization that is working for children and bring them under one roof to do the job better.

I'm not very good at making long-winded, intellectual, academic lectures. Because I've had to sit through so many of those myself, I swore I'd never perpetrate that act of violence on anyone, so I'm not going to do it to you. I'll probably speak a little less than twenty minutes. I would, however, like to say a very special thank-you to a person that I love with all my heart. Her name is Michele Bohana. Thank you, Michie, for bringing us together. And to Jeffrey and to Bryan, this is an incredible event. From the bottom of my heart, I thank you. Bryan, I met your wife last night. She's gorgeous.

This is what the children tell me. I wrote it based on the testimonies I have heard over the past twenty-three years. It's called the Universal Declaration of the Rights of the World's Children:

> We, the children of the world, assert our inalienable right to be heard and have a political voice at the United Nations and at the highest levels of government worldwide. We, the children of the world, must live with justice, with peace and freedom, but above all, with the dignity we deserve. We, the children of the world, require a Marshall Plan, a Geneva Convention, and a World Children's Court of Human Rights which meets regularly to listen to our testimonies and know what is actually happening to us. We intend to provide our own testimonies. We, the children of the world, demand the right to be taken to safe shelters in situations of war. We, the children of the world, consider hunger, disease, forced labor, and all forms of abuse and exploitation perpetrated upon us to be acts of war. And we, the children of the world, until this day, have had no voice. We demand such a voice. We, the children of the world, will develop our own leadership and set an example that will show governments how to live with peace and freedom. We, the children of the world, serve notice on our abusers and exploiters, whoever they may be, that from this day forward, we will begin holding you responsible for our suffering.

Thank you very much.

Discussion Among the Participants

Julian Bond: Two more Irish citizens just received the Nobel Prize, and the nation has demonstrated at the ballot box that it wants to move ahead. What more must be done to put this behind the Irish people?

Betty Williams: I meant to mention that, but I get so nervous that sometimes I forget what I need to say. One of my great friends in the world is a man called John Hume, who has worked ceaselessly and tirelessly for justice and freedom and peace in my country. The other man, David Trimble—it's rather like the Mandela/de Klerk affair, where David Trimble actually managed to push that envelope. Someday, Your Grace, he will shake hands with Gerry Adams. I think right now they have to stop posturing. They're posturing at each other. I was home very recently, and one of the greatest things that we have in our Assembly in Northern Ireland now—there's a women's group in there—and while all the men are posturing at each other, the Women's Coalition is actually doing the work. And so the posturing will stop, too. The absence of violence is only the beginning of the work for peace. We have come a long way in Northern Ireland, and we will go that other mile to sustain the justice and peace we so richly deserve.

Jody Williams: I have a question directed not just to Betty, but to Rigoberta, to Archbishop Tutu, to e verybody whose children have grown up in a culture of violence. The words you say about the voice of children, I certainly support. I worked with Madame Graca Machel, former first lady of Mozambique, currently the wife of Nelson Mandela, when she was the expert at the U.N. to look at the impact of armed conflict on children. I worked in El Salvador, in and out, for many years, and if I remember my statistics correctly, 85 percent of all families were directly affected by the violence in El Salvador. How do you create havens—and this was a great question we had in the Machel project—how do you create havens for children?

But even worse than creating a haven in the midst of conflict, what is the legacy for a country when 85 percent of its families have directly felt violence, when children have grown up in a state of conflict where that is all they know—where they learn that violence is the quickest way, at least seems to be the quickest way, to resolve conflict. How do you undo this so that you really can reestablish the values, reestablish citizenship and good governance? It's just an ongoing question. Olara Otunno[1] and I just had a big debate about this in Belgium. How do you do it?

Betty Williams: I can only speak for Northern Ireland; I am not an expert on the world—I can only speak for a situation that I saw. I already referred to one of the greatest examples, Lagan College. What we actually had to do in that situation was to educate children to educate their parents. The child became the teacher at home. The morning we opened Lagan College, we had eleven students. We were a Protestant short—we had six Catholics and five Protestants. And we were very aware that the media would concentrate on the fact that we didn't have even numbers. About three minutes before the school opened, this woman arrived with her child, and I said to her, "I hate to ask you this, but what's your religion?" She said, "I'm a Protestant," and I hugged her so hard, I nearly broke her ribs. "Thank you, God!" That school now has 1,400 pupils and a waiting list *in utero*. So, it has to start somewhere, Jody. You cannot go out to a child in the Northern Irish situation and take the gun out of his hand or take the bomb out of his hand, without replacing it with something. It has to be replaced with something. And so, we replaced violence with education. We are now seeing the results of this all these years later. There are no quick solutions, love; you and I both know this. It has to be worked for on a daily basis.

---

1. Under-Secretary General, Special Representative of the Secretary General for Children and Armed Conflict, at the United Nations.

Dr. Rigoberta Menchú Tum: In the first place, I would like to say that a huge problem throughout the world is street children. Street children, the children of adolescent mothers, or those who don't have a regular family life, suffer not only from situations of actual violence but from the lack of sensitivity on the part of other people in their society toward them. In terms of the experience that we have of conflicts in Guatemala and in Central America and in Chiapas—in all those areas—none of the peace accords have remembered in any way whatsoever that there are children living in those places; there have been no provisions for children in those peace accords. When those wars came to an end, it was as though there were no orphans in those countries—everything was going to simply come back to normal.

After the peace accords in Guatemala, we have had to begin to struggle to have a code for children so that we can begin to defend the interests of the orphans. Much to our surprise, we found a wall of opposition on the part of those in our country who sell children. It seemed as if we were confronting a new struggle, almost as though the old armed struggle that we had just overcome did not have anything to do with this new stage in the struggle.

I believe very much in local struggles and in national struggles, and I think that in each nation we have to create laws and conditions which will protect the interests of children. I don't think that this can start at the global level. I, too, have spent many, many years going from one international conference to another, and I find that in those international conferences, people do not really know what is going on at different national levels; so we really have to start from the national and then proceed to the global.

Betty Williams: I think, Rigoberta, we have to create a model refuge. As Jody was saying, until we build the model—and I believe all the laureates should be involved in this—of a safe haven and allow the children's voice to be stronger than ours, we will see no changes.

Dr. Rigoberta Menchú Tum: What I understand is that all human beings of this earth have mothers, and if all of us who are the mothers of the world get together, we will create a better world.

Betty Williams: Absolutely. Hear! Hear! I must tell this to His Holiness, whom I also love. I am surrounded by men that I just adore, this is great! When we opened our school, Your Holiness, as you know, our children were educated Catholic or Protestant and really were not aware that there were other religions in the world. So we decided we would bring the other religions in to talk to our children. And one day, I said, "We're bringing in a Buddhist monk today to speak to you," and a little boy said to me, "Is he a Catholic Buddhist or a Protestant Buddhist?"

Archbishop Desmond Tutu: I am not a Buddhist! [*Laughter*] Really, just two things. One is—and I am not trying to be politically correct—to underscore what Betty and Rigoberta were saying. Sitting for two and a half years or so, listening to gruesome accounts of the sorts of things that have taken place in our country from all sides, it struck me more forcibly than I had ever been able to realize that, in fact, we would not have got our liberation without the women. They have been quite, quite extraordinary. Anyone looking at the statistics of our Truth and Reconciliation Commission would be struck by the fact that when men came to testify to the commission, almost always they were testifying about what happened to themselves, but when women came, almost equally, they were telling stories about what happened to somebody else. There was this kind of nurturing—women have nurtured our freedom. We need to give a very special place to them in our struggle, which we probably don't always do.

The second point is that, in a sense, the impact of conflict on children is like what happens with landmines. The effect continues long after the conflict has ceased. Our children, who are going to be the adults of tomorrow, are brutalized. They have lost in many ways a reverence for life, and the violence that then erupts in a society is, in part, the consequence of children having known *nothing better.* They have gone through life seeing people say that the way you resolve a quarrel, a disagreement, is dispatch your enemy—that the best kind of enemy is a dead enemy. And we are going to have to be dealing with that at home. How do you rehabilitate youngsters who had to fight for the right to be human and, in the process, have lost the compassions and the gentlenesses and the reverences for life that ought to be natural to children?

Jody Williams: May I tell a little story? When I worked in El Salvador, we brought wounded children to the United States for donated medical treatment. I met a young woman—she was sixteen, a guerrilla. It was very curious to watch her—the different sides of this woman who felt that she had no option but to take up arms, and I'll tell you why she had to: when she was eleven years old, she came home to her village and she heard the screams of her brother. She hid, but unfortunately, she could see the death squad killing her brother, and they were doing it by skinning him alive. She did not take up arms yet. She finally decided she had no option and no voice in this country when the death squad came back and killed both of her parents. By then, she was thirteen or fourteen. At that point, she decided that it was either pick up a gun, or die herself, and it was also pick up a gun so that no other people would have to watch their brother be skinned in front of them. So what does it mean—childhood—in this kind of situation? But then, I also saw her flirting—I saw this young woman when we brought her to the States—because she had been rehabilitated, if you will, and she needed treatment—I watched her flirting and trying to figure out how a young teenage girl experiences all the other things in life that she was seeing by being in the United States that she had never experienced in El Salvador. It just profoundly affected me—all of her lost childhood and here the adolescence she was trying to recapture in her new experience in the United States. This was juxtaposed with a young woman who had to take up weapons to defend herself, her village, and her dead family. Rigoberta would certainly understand this. How do you deal with that? I totally agree with your analogy; it's a landmine that will affect them forever.

Betty Williams: Jody, you deal with it by changing it. Giving the children their own voice is how you deal with it. There are no answers from adults. We have screwed it up royally for the children of the world, and we need to fix that. There's a young man in Canada named Craig Kildenberger. I don't know whether any of you have heard of him, but he read an article about a Pakistani child who was used in slave labor, and it moved him so much that he persuaded his parents to take him to Pakistan, where he met with this child. He saw the slave labor that was going on. When he came back to Canada—this young man at this stage, Father Tutu, was only eleven, he's fifteen now—challenged his own government on bringing in goods from Pakistan that had been produced through forced labor. And he challenged them so well, and so articulately. You see, children have tremendous brains, but we don't give them credit for that. Mothers will relate to this: when my children were nine, ten, and eleven, they could outsmart me, outwit me, outfox me, outrun me. They're clever, they're really smart, and when Craig came back and challenged his own prime minister, he did it very publicly. And he changed that situation for the children in Pakistan. The Canadians no longer import those rugs. So children can do it, Jody. We just have to give them the way to do it.

Julian Bond: Who else can answer this difficult question: How do you restore humanity to people who may have lost their humanity in the struggle to gain their humanity? How can this be done? Bishop Tutu, is this occurring in South Africa as a result of the work you've been doing?

Archbishop Desmond Tutu: I thought I was raising that problem! [*Laughter*] Sometimes, it is very distressing. It is distressing. You've got to have the organs of civil society seeking to permeate society with the right kind of values. At home, just now, they've had a Moral Summit, in which the leadership of the various religious communities—Christian, Muslim, Jewish, etc.—and political leaders as well as leaders in other spheres of life have come and said, "We've lost a lot of things in the struggle. We've lost the sense of worth of people. We've got to try to recover the art of being human." The whole business about morality, trying to remind people that, in fact, this is a moral universe. That right and wrong, in fact, matter. That you might get away with many things, wrong things; you could succeed, but you will get your comeuppance. It's that kind of universe. But it's not something that you proclaim just by word of mouth. It's got to be incarnated in people. You've got to have structures that assist people in realizing actually that this is a universe ultimately hospitable to gentleness, to compassion, to love, to caring, to sharing, and that there ought to be people who are willing to live for that. Then children will, I hope, catch on.

A lot of things have gone wrong at home, as some things have gone right. And so, whilst we celebrate, there are other things that we realize have gone wrong, and as I grow more decrepit, I realize that there are some extraordinary truths that people usually might have pooh-poohed, but are for real—that there is no reason whatsoever to assume that because I was involved in a just struggle, and I had my idealisms, that when I win the struggle, I will necessarily maintain those idealisms. There actually is something—it's not a myth—called "original sin." Each one of us has constantly got to be saying, "There, but for the grace of God, go I."

Betty Williams: Original sin. Mortal sin and venial sins, I used to get so confused as a child. I think I commit mortal sins constantly, because I am constantly angry about what's happening to the children. Anger is an emotion that can be very destructive, and I have to be very careful about my anger and direct it correctly. I want to say this for the students in the audience because His Grace is here; I am a great believer in getting you involved—put your money where your mouth is—and we're doing a project for South Africa. I was with His Grace earlier in the year when we did a Peace Jam on Robben Island where we brought young people together from Capetown and surrounding areas. And it was a wonderful experience, Your Grace. You gave them back a lot of what they'd lost, in just some of the things that you said to them. We had a young girl come up to us at the end of the Peace Jam, and she was a very tiny little girl—[*to Archbishop Tutu*] do you remember, Your Grace?— and she said, "Mama Williams" (and I was crying, they called me Mama Williams), "I have been raped," [*to Archbishop Tutu*] do you remember, Your Grace? I went to His Grace and I said, "Your Grace, there's a child here that's just been raped," and His Grace came over, and we did what we could for her. But we went to a school in Mannenberg, which has over one thousand students, about two books in the library, and no computers. I want to get the students here involved in helping me bring computers to the school in Mannenberg. Will you do that? Hands up, I want your name, your address, your date of birth, your telephone number— on a piece of paper, please, because that's a project that we are now doing at World Centers of Compassion for Children. Tears without action are wasted sentiment. We're going to take out twenty computers to the Mannenberg School and ten to the city of Capetown.

Bobby Muller: One of the very encouraging things in my experience is the resilience of the human spirit. I am just going to share a little bit of a personal thing that happened. I considered myself a very righteous guy, a very good guy. When I went into the Marine Corps, I was really sensitive to kids. I went through the whole training thing, went to Vietnam. Vietnam was a very confusing war. You didn't have a front line, and you didn't have a clear identification of who your enemy was. I had a lot of situations—I was a platoon commander—where I had my guys out doing operations, and the enemy often would have the kids come in, and we'd give them C-rations, we'd give them stuff. A couple of times on the same night, we would get hit, attacked. Our command post and critical positions were obviously known to the attacking force, the Viet Cong. It turned out that it was the kids whom we had befriended and given the C-rats to, etc., that had gotten their brothers to come in and attack us that night. A lot of things happened in my interaction with the Vietnamese. We used to have these heating tabs that we would light up and they would burn with an invisible flame to cook up the C-rats. At one point, we were on a truck convoy going down the highway, and my guys were lighting up these heating tabs and throwing them off the truck. They were a valued little commodity; so the kids would come out of the villages and pick up these heating tabs. Being that they had an invisible flame, the kids couldn't tell that they had been lit up, and it would stick to their hand, their fingers, and burn them. And I remember laughing at that.

When I got shot, I was medevacked to a hospital ship, and they had me in intensive care for several days, and they had a psychiatrist come and talk to me. He said, "Is there anything you want to talk about?" He was presumably inquiring about the fact that I was going to be a paraplegic. My question to him was: "Two days before, I had sat down, chowed down and had a big lunch amongst a whole bunch of dead bodies, and it meant nothing to me. Is there something wrong with me?" He said, "No, there's nothing wrong with you. You've been in an extraordinary circumstance, and your mind has automatic defense mechanisms that come into play to allow you to get through these extraordinary circumstances." He said, "You go back to New York City, and next year when you see somebody get hit by a cab, you're going to be as affected as anybody else." This is exactly what happened.

What I am saying to you is that I think people are inherently good. I think the power of love and the power of good is a very, very strong force. But, we can be affected by the negative, we can be affected by the forces of, for lack of a better term, darkness. Due to being on the ground and getting involved in a situation of killing people and having my guys killed, I sometimes say that I took a little bit of a walk down that path of darkness. I personally realized how a good guy could wind up doing unconscionable things and have a value structure fundamentally altered. Remember My Lai, O.K.? In My Lai, it was the good guys—it was an American infantry unit that went in and murdered 504 Vietnamese women and children and old people, without one single shot being fired in return. That was the good guys. O.K.?

What I am saying may not be clear, but when you get exposed to evil and when you get into darkness and the circumstances around you are of that nature, they can have an affect on anyone. Some of you may say, "That could never happen to me." Well, let me tell you something: you're kidding yourself! I didn't think it could happen to me. I was shocked when I realized it did happen. But, the positive part of the story, to wrap it up, is that by coming back, by getting love, getting nurturing, getting out of where the forces of darkness and the negative energy of basic evil can work on you, allows you the opportunity to rehabilitate, to rejuvenate. I've seen it with literally hundreds of veterans who were exposed to the most horrific combat—I have seen it with kids, I've seen it with a lot of people in war zones that I have gone to. We have a rejuvenative capability—stop feeding the negative, take them out of those situations, provide love, give them a decent environment, and even with those that have been crushed, you can so oftentimes bring them back to wholeness and to health.

Betty Williams: Absolutely. There's just one more thing that I'd like to add. I am a Catholic, and I challenge my church on blessing men to go to war. I think we have to challenge the leadership of whatever church we belong to. Remove padres from armies.

Questions from the Audience

Jeffrey Hopkins: This question is addressed to Harn Yawnghwe. How would you educate the children affected by oppression and war to grow up *not* to retaliate?

Harn Yawnghwe: To give a short answer: It is not an easy process, because as everybody has been saying, when they see the suffering, when they experience it themselves, it's very hard not to want to have revenge. It is necessary to create a better environment, a better atmosphere. In the case of Burma, I am hopeful that it will be possible through solving the political problems. The military has been trying to solve it by using violence. What we are saying is that this will not solve the problem; you have to resolve political problems through political means. Hopefully, that kind of thinking—also what José has been talking about in East Timor, not to take revenge on the Indonesian migrant workers—I think that is the way we need to go.

Jeffrey Hopkins: This is a question for His Holiness the Dalai Lama. Can the religions worldwide, given their dissimilarities and their followers' different passions, act as a coherent force in the peace process?

His Holiness the Dalai Lama: My belief is that the various religious traditions have great potential to increase compassion, the sense of caring for one another, and the spirit of reconciliation. However, I believe that a human being, without religious faith, can be a very good person—sincere, a good heart, having a sense of caring for others—without belief in a particular religious faith.

In Christianity, Islam, and Judaism as well as in many other religious traditions, the concept of a creator is very powerful, very effective, and then in some other religious traditions like Buddhism and Jainism there is no Creator God; oneself is almost like a creator—self-creation. That also is a very powerful method to transform our attitudes. Both types approach more or less the same goal through different methods, different ways. I am not talking about heaven or other final states, but simply about becoming a good human being, a warm-hearted person. Of course, all religious traditions have this potential.

However, we also need another sort of spirituality without any religious faith but simply, I feel, on the basis of awareness. [*To José Ramos-Horta*] You mentioned that the ultimate source of conflict is ignorance. I think that for all trouble, there are a lot of causes and conditions. Some are very substantial causes, and among them ignorance, lack of awareness, is the ultimate, root cause. Then other different factors or conditions also contribute. However, the causes and conditions of violence can be counteracted through education, through analyzing, "What use is violence? Does violence ultimately benefit yourself? Ah, it brings more violence, counter-violence. And eventually, there is mutual destruction." Repeated reflection in this way undermines the impetus to violence.

On the other hand, a certain amount of disagreement, or different views and contradictions, is always present. Even if, day by day, we wage war continuously, contradictions will not be resolved. They will always remain. Different ideas, different economic reasons, and sources of conflict always remain. Think about this reality: "Even if I use violence intensively, the problem cannot be solved; it persists. Instead, there will be mutual destruction, mutual suffering."

So then, we have to solve problems, but through other means: dialogue, compromise. [*To Archbishop Tutu*] You are a great preacher! The spirit of reconciliation: fully respect others' views, and others' rights, and develop a sense of genuine concern about others' welfare and their right. And then compromise. Only compromise. That's the only way.

So you see, through awareness, these attitudes can develop without any religious faith or religious belief. Therefore, I usually call them basic human values. These are the good qualities of human nature. [*To Bobby Muller*] In just the way that you mentioned, I am very much encouraged—there are a lot of bads in our emotions, but our ultimate nature is, I believe, gentleness. Everyone has the seed of a sense of commitment, a sense of responsibility, a sense of caring for one another.

Of course, I believe that the various different religious traditions also have great potential. So, let us try to utilize that potential. Shall we? Thank you.

Jeffrey Hopkins: This is a question for President Arias. Is it easier to identify the problems and motive forces behind religious and ethnic hatred than it is to speak against the horrific results of multinational capitalism?

President Oscar Arias Sánchez: I believe in the market economy. I don't see how capitalism has anything to do with what we are talking about here. I am a strong believer in democracy, as well as in the market economy, as well as in political pluralism, etc. The problem is that even though Marxism and Communism have been buried, and both are dead, that doesn't mean that democracy has triumphed. Democracy is not an end in itself. We all know that for more than 2,000 years, democracy has been a means. The end is always the human being—the mother, the child. As long as democracy does not deliver the goods—and democracy is not delivering the goods in many or most African countries, in many Latin American countries, in many Asian countries—so eventually it is going to be questioned. Democracy is going to be questioned by the people, by societies: "Why do we need to praise and struggle for democracy if democracy is creating more and more and more injustice, and poverty increases every day, and inequality increases every day, etc., etc.?"

It was Berdiaev, the Russian thinker, who said, "The problem with Christianity is the Christians." And this is true for all religions; *we* are the ones who are failing—our indifference. I don't think we can enjoy peace in the twenty-first century with our ethics of the twentieth century. It has been mentioned here that the twentieth century has been the bloodiest century in the history of humankind. I mean, how can we enjoy peace, security, and freedom with the values that have prevailed? Selfishness instead of solidarity, so much greed, so much cynicism, so much hypocrisy. I will be speaking tomorrow—perhaps this might sound too strong—about the cynicism of this great nation. I think there is a need for the United States to lead, because the world expects leadership from Washington. But in the right way. Politics goes hand in hand with responsibility and with morality. Certainly by sending arms to so many countries in the world, you are not taking the moral decisions that you should. This country taught the rest of the world that "Right is might," and that's what the world expects from this great nation.

So, trying to answer your question, I think that the reason why we might not enjoy a more peaceful future is simply because we, as individuals, have failed. There is need for a new ethics; otherwise, it is going to be very difficult to enjoy peace. I think there is need for more compassion, for more generosity, for more solidarity, for more tolerance, and certainly for more love.

Dr. Rigoberta Menchú Tum

Guatemala

Short Biography

Rigoberta Menchú Tum was born on January 9, 1959, in the Guatemalan village of Chimal. Her father, Vicente Menchú, was a community leader, and her mother, Juana Tum, was a midwife and healer. The family was Quiché, one of twenty-one Mayan groups living in Guatemala.

Political turmoil plagued Guatemala since the country gained its independence in 1821. Except for one ten-year stretch of representative government, which began in 1945, the nation had endured years of right-wing dictatorships, insurgencies, coups, and periods of military rule. One significant revolt occurred the year after Menchú Tum was born. In 1960 junior military officers rose up against General Ydigoras Fuentes, the nation's autocratic leader. Failing in their attempt, the officers went into hiding in the Guatemalan mountains, where they formed left-wing guerrilla groups that would wage armed insurrections against the government for the next thirty-six years. In retaliation, right-wing groups formed to mete out vigilante justice to anyone suspected of leftist activities. The Guatemalan countryside became a dangerous place, and the people who lived in the countryside—primarily ethnic minorities—were caught in the middle of the warring.

Instilled with a sense of injustice at a young age, Menchú Tum and her brothers joined the Committee of Peasant Unity in 1979. This group, known by its Spanish abbreviation of CUC, had been founded by her father and other village leaders. Its members became targets of the army and vigilantes. Betrayed by a villager, her sixteen-year-old brother, Petrocinio, was captured in September 1979, then tortured and executed. Less than five months later, her father and other activists were killed inside the Spanish Embassy by Guatemalan soldiers. Only three months after that, her mother was kidnapped, raped, and tortured before being left to die on a remote hillside. Her village was razed. Fearing for her life, Menchú Tum fled to Mexico, where she came under the protection of the Catholic Guatemalan Church-in-Exile and lived for the next twelve years.

Determined to restore basic rights to indigenous peoples, she became active in the work of the United Nations. In 1982, she helped establish a U.N. working group on indigenous populations. She attended U.N. General Assembly sessions and participated in the U.N.'s Commission on Human Rights from 1983 to 1995.

For her efforts on behalf of indigenous people worldwide, she was awarded the Nobel Peace Prize in 1992. At age thirty-three, she was the youngest person ever to receive this honor. "By maintaining a disarming humanity in a brutal world, Rigoberta Menchú Tum appeals to the best in all of us, wherever we live and whatever our background," said Francis Sejersted, chairman of the Norwegian Nobel Committee, in conferring the honor. "She stands as a uniquely potent symbol of a just struggle. There is a most urgent need to define the rights of aboriginal peoples and to respect those rights in a manner which makes it possible to live in peace and mutual understanding," he added. "To succeed in this, we need people like Rigoberta Menchú Tum."

Ironically, Menchú Tum's prize was conferred five hundred years after Christopher Columbus's "discovery" of the New World. As history has shown, the resulting colonization of the Americas was rarely respectful of the basic rights of the indigenous people living on these lands. The same has proven true of colonization efforts in other areas of the world as well.

Using the monetary award from the Nobel Peace Prize, in January 1993 she founded the Rigoberta Menchú Tum Foundation. Its goals include defending and promoting the rights and values of indigenous peoples, offering peace education, and promoting sustainable development. To date, the foundation has helped thousands of exiled Guatemalans return to their homeland.

Also in 1993, Menchú Tum became the goodwill ambassador of the U.N.'s International Year of the Indigenous Peoples. As part of the U.N.'s Second Worldwide Conference on Human Rights, she organized the First Summit of the Indigenous Peoples, which was held in May 1993 in Chimaltenango, Guatemala, and attended by the indigenous leaders of many countries. She also organized the Second Summit of the Indigenous Peoples, which was held five months later in Oaxtepec, Morelos, Mexico.

Currently, she is the goodwill ambassador for UNESCO's International Decade of the Indigenous Peoples of the World, as well as president of the Indigenous Initiative for Peace. This latter organization is working to protect indigenous people's rights, establish judicial processes for acknowledging and protecting these rights, and promote peaceful resolutions to controversies affecting indigenous peoples.

Additionally, Menchú Tum is a member of the PeaceJam Foundation advisory council and a counselor to Federico Mayor Zaragoza, general director of UNESCO. She has received seventeen honorary doctorate degrees from universities around the world. In June 1998, she received the Prince of Asturias Award for

International Cooperation. Her book, *Crossing Borders,* was published in English in 1998.

"What I treasure most in life is being able to dream," Rigoberta Menchú Tum has said. "During my most difficult moments and complex situations, I have been able to dream of a more beautiful future."

DR. RIGOBERTA MENCHÚ TUM
"The Role of Indigenous People in a Democratic Guatemala"

[Dr. Rigoberta Menchú Tum's remarks begin with a sentence in Mayan, after which she says through her interpreters,[2] "There is no translation." The remainder of her presentation is translated from Spanish.]

I don't know what I will say today after listening to so many experiences, and after being among so many extraordinary people, including Bishop Desmond Tutu and the Dalai Lama. Bishop Desmond Tutu has been my role model for a long time, and I feel very well accompanied, spiritually. Since I will be using a translator, I understand that I will be allowed to speak forty minutes!

The great inspiration of my work is the indigenous peoples, maybe because I am Maya and I also was born in a country where indigenous peoples have been the majority and where we have made history, have had to make war, and have to make peace. Over and above feeling indigenous, I believe that the indigenous peoples of the world are a fount of inspiration for an intercultural world. The indigenous peoples have a message to give in the prevention of conflict because for many centuries, our peoples used dialogue, patient conversation toward peaceful means, for the resolution of interethnic, familial, and intercultural problems.

---

2. Her interpreters were Herbert "Tico" Braun, Professor of History; Ricardo Padron, Assistant Professor of Spanish; and Alejandra Maudet, Assistant Director of the Hispanic Studies Program at the University of Virginia.

Overall, the contribution of the indigenous peoples is toward a new perspective on education, one of education in the word—education in which the value of the word will give the opportunity to the other to express himself or herself and to be heard. I want to say that to us was given, as a people—not as famous men and women, but as a people—an experience of dialogue, an experience of conversation to solve internal problems. We were able to contribute to peace, to negotiation, and, thank God, we were able to contribute so that the war would come to an end in Central America—but from a collective conviction, as a raw, painful experience, as part of the victims of armed conflict.

We've also contributed to peace as exiles, as displaced people, as refugees, and from the standpoint of indigenous women and indigenous peoples, who are not always listened to, not only in our country but also throughout the world. We learned that dialogue and negotiation belonged to the elite. They were the ones who had dialogue at their disposal, the ones who could decide what could be done with dialogue. We can also say that it was their decision to bring the war to an end. In the case of Guatemala, if the agents in the war had decided twenty years ago to speak with each other, then we would have prevented thousands and thousands of deaths, we would have avoided a great deal of destruction. It is important that the actors in the war must decide to seek peace, and this is important throughout the world, not just in our own case. Right now, we are reconstructing our country in the midst of great difficulties. Especially when there has been so much distrust, so much social fragmentation and especially when the system of justice has always favored certain groups, it has been a great struggle to create a just legal system.

I also come here to seek allies. Will and desire are not enough to bring about change. Change is brought about by societies, by institutions, by governments. Changes are something that we all make together. Throughout the world, indigenous peoples have not only not changed their situation, but they are running the risk of becoming reduced to indigenous ghettos. I struggle to break that silence. I call out to you so that you will recognize that indigenous peoples have an intercultural experience, a multiethnic experience, a diverse experience.

I also struggle so that together we can erase all the stereotypes that exist about indigenous peoples. When indigenous peoples are overprotected, this overprotection is also racism. If we forget them, and they are marginalized, that is also racism. The problem is that we never know which is worse—forgetting or too much attention. People want to know what I think about Chiapas, what I think about Colombia, what I think about Guatemala. But I want to say that the most important thing is to do continuous work. We want to make a contribution to intercultural education, to a culture of peace, in which peace does not just come as a result of war but rather as the product of peaceful coexistence, and of exchange, and the result of mutual respect. We must accept that today's world is a multiethnic world, a multilinguistic world, a multicultural world. If we don't accept that, we will always be playing to the dominant cultures.

When I am in an indigenous community in Bolivia, in Ecuador, in Guatemala, in Mexico, I can see that misery and poverty are not the sole property of indigenous peoples, but of many, many people throughout the world. When I see the street children, I notice that not many of them are indigenous. Why? Because the children are in the community, they are in the family, because they have found a new family. The same thing has happened with indigenous children in the areas of conflict. All the orphans of the indigenous people have been absorbed by their own community. The indigenous people in the areas of conflict found a new home in the community, but in other conflicts not involving indigenous peoples, I have found that orphaned children have been left out on the street.

This is to say that indigenous peoples have a lesson to offer in the prevention of conflicts and the resolution of conflicts. We also have a message in the reconciliation of our peoples. In order to do so, we have to create a different climate, a climate of respect toward us. Each time that we have common problems, we must find common solutions. This is why I am here with my colleagues, my fellow Nobel Laureates. I believe that each of us has a specialty in our own work, in our own convictions, that works in favor of peace. When we struggle individually, we sometimes give it an accent—more Maya, more woman, more radical, less radical— but we are all working toward the same goal.

Finally, I would like to say that we have in our hands the possibility to start the new millennium with good intentions or to turn to the new millennium simply observing the problems of the world. We have no need for observers in this world; we need actors. We need people who will work, who will know how to make speeches—but only once in a while. Also, we need people who will struggle, no matter under what conditions, for collective values. I want to convoke you then, so we can all find one thing that we can do in the new millennium. For example, the University of Virginia could give scholarships to five thousand Guatemalan students, Mayas!

Well, I don't want to tell you what you can give, but you have to give all that you can give. Conviction is not enough. It is not enough to be conscious of the problems of the world; how we involve ourselves in their solution is the most important thing. So, let us once again believe in the children, in the youth. Let us once again believe in indigenous peoples. Let us once again believe in the people who can promote dialogue in search for peace. And, of course, let us all struggle to get rid of firearms, for as long as there are arms, there will be people who will use them.

Thank you very much for this, and I await your questions.

Discussion Among the Participants

Julian Bond: What is the responsibility of a state where there are competing and emerging ethnic or religious minorities striving for recognition, some degree of independence? How does a state balance the needs of these groups with its desire for stability and homogeneity among its people?

Dr. Rigoberta Menchú Tum: I think that there is a legal matter that has to be addressed, a question of laws and a change in constitutions in a country like that. All of the national constitutions recognize a homogenous people; they refer to only one national culture and do not speak of the multiple ethnic groups that exist within one nation. Maybe there was a point in time in history where dominant cultures had the right or the ability to dominate others, but that is no longer the case today, and this has to be changed because today everybody is multicultural, multilingual, and multiethnic. And if there is a form of education that exists that goes against a culture, it means that it is not an education at all.

So, I think there are formal and legal changes that must be made, but that which is most difficult is to change the attitude that people have, because there also are countries and constitutions with wonderful laws that have never been enforced. In Guatemala, in the peace process, we have managed to produce a series of wonderful laws that recognize the different ethnic and indigenous groups of the country, but those accords will take a long, long time—many, many years—before they can be implemented. But the world believed that the dove of peace had landed on our heads, that peace had arrived, and that everything was fine and nothing much more had to be done in order to accomplish peace. Therefore, I think that much has to be done educationally from a perspective of multicultural identities.

Many people have said to me, "Well, what happens if we give indigenous peoples technology, will they lose their culture?" What

I say to them is, "Don't worry so much about what we will gain and what we will lose. Just give it to us, and we will use it." But if those technologies are imposed on us, and they do not serve our interests, our communities will reject them with all our energy, as we have always done. But if our peoples incorporate those technologies into our own cultures, with our own knowledge, with our own local technologies, then, certainly, those things that are offered to us and given to us will have many positive results, will save many lives, and will offer a dignified life for the people. So if there are some rich people here, and some big corporations, they, too, can work with indigenous peoples as long as it is in a relationship of trust and understanding.

In the last three decades—I am a very young person, so I don't know very much of what has happened before those three decades—I have to say that many governments have simply refused to take a positive attitude and to begin to discuss questions about native peoples and indigenous cultures in their own countries. Or ethnic minorities. Or religious peoples. One of the big fears that immediately emerges is that people say, "Well, if we give these people more rights, they will suddenly want to become independent." It appears that our independence within nations is what people worry the most about, but I think that in our day and age there are very, very serious problems with the lack of comprehension, the lack of understanding, amongst people of different ethnic and religious orientations. It is a very serious problem that has to be on our agenda, and we have to engage it. In addition, I would like to struggle to be a bishop, and a cardinal, although I don't think I am going to be successful in that!

Julian Bond: Earlier today, you were discussing your contacts with the insurgencies in Nicaragua, Colombia, and Chiapas, and saying there was a difference between Colombia and Nicaragua, the insurgencies there, and Chiapas. Can you talk about that?

Dr. Rigoberta Menchú Tum: There is a deep difference between the insurgencies that took place in Central America and the conflict that is currently taking place in Chiapas. Also, the peace process is very, very different between Central America and Chiapas. In Central America, there were two parties in conflict: on the one side, the insurgency, and on the other, the state and the military. There were no other actors. One of the big problems was the militarization of state power in those countries. But in Chiapas, there are many different actors and many different places where conflict occurs. This means that the solution in Chiapas will not be easy.

In Guatemala, it unfortunately took ten years of dialogue to reach the point of peace accords. It is important that something like that happens in Chiapas, because otherwise the situation will become more complicated, and we will have a situation like that in Colombia today. It is a frontier area, rich in resources, where people are struggling over those resources. Indigenous peoples live there, but this is not an indigenous struggle, because many different peoples live in Chiapas. Simply by recognizing that there are many different actors involved, and not just two basic parties in conflict, we begin to recognize what needs to be done. If you are on the Internet, you can always ask me more questions at my website.

Jody Williams: What is the current situation of groups who struggle to have a voice in the socio-political life of Guatemala? Have they had to lower their voice to maintain peace on the surface, or do they still struggle with the same determination to make sure that the beautiful words of peace on paper are a reality for everybody in society?

Dr. Rigoberta Menchú Tum: So that you don't hear me as being very pessimistic, I am going to say some of the most optimistic things that I believe. The most important goal that we have accomplished in Guatemala is to bring violent conflict to an end—conflict of thirty-seven years that created all kinds of separate interests. A war from which many people made their living, earned their daily income and made a lot of money, as well. So it is a very good thing that the war is over. But we have not all won; those who are most affected are the victims of the war: the internal refugees that are probably 95 percent indigenous peoples, as well as the former combatants on both sides—on the side of the government, of the military, and of the guerrillas. Those combatants have not obtained or gotten anything. They are no longer mobilized, they are no longer members of groups, but we find that they do not have anything; they don't have land or a way to earn their income; they are looking for some way to survive.

Since Jody Williams knows El Salvador, and we make comparisons, we often feel that more has been accomplished in El Salvador than in Guatemala. But what has been obtained, what we have managed to get in El Salvador, really is quite minimal. In Guatemala, we are still struggling to streamline the judicial system, and if I were to tell you just one case of trying to get a legal judicial process going against the military, you would recognize how difficult and complex that is. There are still judges being bought, there are threats, blackmail. Peace accords are political agreements, and political agreements have to become judicial agreements, and to go from law to actual practice is a long process. We are changing the entire police system—we are trying to change the army from being repressive to non-repressive. All of this will take a long period of time. We, the indigenous peoples, it appears, are absent from all of this. We are absent in the sense that we are absent among the elite, among those who are making the decisions, but we are very active in all other regards. Many changes are taking place. There are indigenous peoples who are local mayors; we are participating all the time in a broader peace process. This has been our struggle—it is not enough simply to sign the peace accords, but what really happens is what occurs after those peace accords have been signed. What is oftentimes worse than the war is the period after the war, to come to grips with the reality of our country, with the repressions which the war has left, and with what it has left us for the future.

Harn Yawnghwe: I would be interested to know whether it is possible, according to your legal system, for somebody like yourself to be in national politics? For example, could you run for president?

Dr. Rigoberta Menchú Tum: Yes, indigenous peoples can participate in the political institutions of the country, but unfortunately they cannot do so as indigenous peoples. So, if someone who is an indigenous person would like to be president of Guatemala, he or she would have to work with an established political party, and that party would have to support the candidate. If it were by indigenous voting, that person would not need a political party. The political parties in the country are all racist, so they will not work for someone who is indigenous. Maybe I am not completely correct here, and there will be a change in the new millennium. So then maybe the question is, "Why don't indigenous peoples themselves form a political party?" [*In English*] *Because we don't have money!* Because we indigenous peoples are the poorest peoples of this earth—we have not had our own businesses, our own developed economies, we have not been able to make our own wealth. In addition, we are not very experienced in the world, in politics; we don't know what the intrigue of politics is, we haven't learned what it is like to trip up another political candidate! And regarding whether I would like to be president of Guatemala, what I can say is that it is the main worry of a lot of people that I do want to be.

Questions from the Audience

Jeffrey Hopkins: This is a question for Archbishop Tutu. What thought, what idea, did you communicate to your country's leaders that finally forced them to action?

Archbishop Desmond Tutu: Quite seriously, I did nothing. There were many other people who were doing superb work. I often say that I was the leader by default, because our real leaders were in jail or in exile, and perhaps it was part of God's sense of humor that God chose to have someone like me. It was probably because I had an easy name!

Jeffrey Hopkins: The next question is for Jody Williams. How do you feel about the trend in anti-affirmative-action legislation that may have the power to eliminate programming designed to inspire minority groups and women toward historically white male dominated careers in academic pursuits?

Jody Williams: The question doesn't have too much to do with landmines, although the question is indeed a landmine. I would prefer to address the overarching question of racism in our society that Betty touched on before. I don't think that racism is the purview of just this country; everywhere you go, you find racism. Look at what's happening in India, between the Muslims and the Hindus. Part of the problem is the political correctness running rampant in the country at this moment, where we pretend there isn't racism. We pretend that we are all the same. I believe that unless and until we can address each other's similarities, but equally our differences, we will never get beyond it. Pretending that we are all the same is absurd; we are not all the same. We are all the same before the law—theoretically. But we don't all have the same skills, we don't all have the same even basic gifts or not-gifts, and as long as we keep pretending that African-American culture is the same as white culture, is the same as Hispanic-American culture, we are never going to bridge the gap. I prefer you come up to me in my face and say, "You're a white American, I'm a black American. We are different. How are we going to deal with the differences and move to respect for each other?"

Additionally, I am a complete believer in personal responsibility. Sentiment without action is irrelevant. I can sit there and cry with the best of them. I can. Italian Catholic—we cry good. Mortal sin—I used to have them all the time. All sin was mortal—burn in hell. Seriously, I used to fear hell. Now I know that hell is on earth, fighting against the evils of the planet. But if we don't take personal responsibility to change the things we don't like, it's going to get worse. If you don't think it should be this way, get up, go out, and change it. Don't sit back and wait for the other guy to defend your right. If you really believe you have one, go for it! You can't sit back and say, "Oh, we know Julian Bond and the NAACP will take care of this because that's their issue area." Excuse me? He is one voice, they are one part of the voice, but you are part of this society, and if you want it different, *make it different.* That's my answer.

Jeffrey Hopkins: This question is addressed to His Holiness the Dalai Lama. Does Your Holiness find from your personal experience that philosophical ideas affect people's behavior? For example, do you see that an overemphasis on oneself, as opposed to an emphasis on helping others, affects one's behavior?

His Holiness the Dalai Lama: I don't know! [*Laughter*] First of all, I don't know what the exact meaning of "philosophy" is. Anyway, a certain way of thinking, vision, viewpoint, or deeper meaning definitely widens our view—our outlook—towards oneself and toward others. For example, the Buddhist view or philosophy of interdependency is very helpful in widening our perspective. It is the theory that one thing depends on many other factors. Once that sort of understanding arises, then when an event occurs, immediately there is a desire to look at the wider implications, or the causes and conditions—to look at these rather than at this event itself. So in this way one's outlook is useful. But otherwise, I don't know.

Jeffrey Hopkins: The next question is for José Ramos-Horta. How does one strike a healthy balance between action on a local level and action on a broader, international scale?

José Ramos-Horta: Both must be intimately linked. There is no escaping that to achieve changes, you have to act locally. A famous American politician said, "All politics are local." That is applicable everywhere, but at the same time in this increasingly small, interconnected world, we cannot isolate ourselves. Often the actions we undertake internationally have a greater impact on the behavior of a certain country than, let's say, the use of violence against that particular country. I have had this experience in dealing with the U.S. Congress in relation to the situation in East Timor or Indonesia. In discussions with some of my colleagues, freedom fighters, I said, "By getting action by the U.S. Congress to ban the delivery of an F-16 aircraft to Indonesia, it is far, far cheaper than if we ever try to shoot down that F-16 once it's delivered. No matter how much money we get, and we'll never get it—we'll never be able to shoot down that F-16 anyway." So, by talking to a few really moral individuals in the U.S. Congress, we managed to cause such an uproar that, in the end, the Indonesians said they got sick and tired of the whole controversy and gave up trying to buy the F-16.

I will give you another example that is just remarkable. Four old women in England—three were British, one Swedish—went into the British Hawk Aircraft factory in Liverpool—they went just with kitchen tools—and damaged the entire computer system of one of the Hawk Aircraft that had been paid for by the Indonesians and was waiting to be delivered to Indonesia. That factory was supposed to be high-security, but somehow they managed to enter, did their job, completed it; they danced around the aircraft, and still the security didn't come. Only when they finally phoned the media and the media arrived, did security come. They were arrested, and I was one of the people who finally was allowed as a defense witness for them in Liverpool. One of the women spoke in court, saying, "I read a statement by José Ramos-Horta about the use of the Hawk aircraft in Timor, and that is why I did this." There I was—she said she was motivated by something I said—I felt *so bad* the entire day because I thought this woman might be sentenced to twelve years in prison because of a statement I issued.

But finally, against all our expectations, they were acquitted. For the first time in a British court, the invocation of an act of conscience was accepted. The trial lawyer for the four women was Gareth Pierce, the same lawyer played by Emma Thompson in the film *In the Name of the Father*. It was a highly successful case, and—according to British aerospace—it set a very dangerous precedent that it is now legal to incapacitate a weapon in England.

That is just to show that in our experience, being a small country at one point abandoned by the major powers, no army behind us—it was international action that gave us the moral boost, support, that gave us the courage, the faith, to continue, and it was solidarity work in the Congress, the European Parliament, and governments, that caused so much damage to the Indonesian side to the point that East Timor became the most costly foreign policy issue for Indonesia.

His Holiness the Dalai Lama: May I add something to my answer to the second part of the earlier question?

Jeffrey Hopkins: Yes, please. If one's idea is too strongly on individualism—your own self—does it make a difference to have that idea, or to have an idea of altruism?

His Holiness the Dalai Lama: Now again, I don't know the exact meaning of "individualism." But in any case, the moment one thinks of oneself, the whole mental focus is very narrow, and within that narrow area, even a small problem appears to be very big.

However, the moment you think about others, your mental outlook becomes very broad. Your own problems appear as insignificant. That is a big difference.

Then, another thing: If we develop a strong sense of caring for others, then when we hear about or see the pain or unfortunate experiences of others, at that moment your peace of mind, or your calm mind, is disturbed a little bit, but then, if you look deeper, this feeling of burden—from a sense of caring for others—is voluntary. *You take care of others. You are taking sincerest concern for others' welfare.* Deep inside, you voluntarily accept it, and, on the basis of that feeling, there is inner strength; you have self-confidence. And on the basis of that, you have the courage to take care of others. The other way: when just thinking, "Myself, myself," if some unfortunate thing happens, it is really overwhelming. So, deep down there are big differences. Thinking about others actually is of great benefit to oneself.

Archbishop Desmond Tutu

South Africa

Short Biography

A social and political system that stifles the talents and dignity of its subjects can unintentionally channel those talents back on itself. Were it not for South African apartheid, Desmond Tutu would have become a doctor or remained a teacher. Instead, he entered the Anglican priesthood and became the head of the Anglican church in South Africa—as well as one of the most powerful and influential opponents of South Africa's repressive and unjust apartheid system.

From the time the Republic of South Africa was formed in 1910 from four separate English and Boer provinces, blacks living in that country had no vote and no real political representation. As early as 1912, the African National Congress was formed to protest the discriminatory nature of the country's national constitution. Some reforms were initiated, but progress halted and then reversed beginning in 1948, when the conservative Afrikaner party won control of the government. In a series of laws that were passed by the National Party, the South African government set up comprehensive restrictions on the rights and freedoms of non-whites that came to be known as apartheid. These laws regulated where blacks could live, where and in what jobs they could work, whom they could visit or associate with, what kind of schooling and medical care they would receive, even whom they could marry. African freehold rights in white areas were largely eliminated, families were split apart, and some three and a half million people were forcibly moved and resettled. Thousands died at the hands of the state security forces. The government could detain without trial anyone suspected of anti-government activity; many critics died in detention under mysterious circumstances.

As a black South African, Desmond Tutu experienced apartheid firsthand. Born on October 7, 1931, in the gold-mining town of Klerksdorp, Tutu was twelve years old when his family moved to Sophiatown, a black township outside of Johannesburg. His father worked as a schoolteacher; his mother, as a cook and domestic servant.

Tutu contracted tuberculosis as a teenager and spent twenty months in bed recuperating. He was able to continue his studies with the help of frequent visits by the white Anglican priest Trevor Huddleston, after whom Tutu's son, Trevor, was later named. Huddleston's articulate and passionate opposition to the apartheid system, and his belief that the brotherhood of man in Jesus Christ was multiracial, influenced the moral development of his young student.

Forsaking a longed-for medical career due to a lack of sufficient funds, Tutu became a high school teacher in 1954. The following year, he married Leah Normalizo, with whom he would eventually have one son and three daughters. He resigned his teaching post in protest in 1957, after the state mandated an inferior education for blacks and criminalized those who attempted to teach more. He next entered an Anglican seminary: "It just occurred to me that, if the Church would have me, the profession of priest could be a good way of serving my people," he later said.

Tutu was ordained in 1961, then moved to London. From 1962 to 1966, he worked part-time as a curate while completing his master's degree in theology from King's College, London. Tutu returned to South Africa for four years to teach theology at various seminaries, then journeyed again to London to serve for three years as associate director of the Theological Education Fund of the World Council of Churches, a position involving extensive international travel. In 1975 Tutu was appointed dean of St. Mary's Cathedral in Johannesburg, followed by his selection the next year as bishop of Lesotho. In 1978, he was appointed general secretary of the South African Council of Churches.

Throughout his career, Tutu steadfastly and courageously spoke out against the South African apartheid system. In his view, the aims and methods of apartheid were diametrically opposed to the Christian gospel of love and unity. Believing that there could be no peace or security in his country until everyone enjoyed the same basic human rights and fundamentals of justice and liberty, he consistently preached a message of love in the face of institutionalized hate.

In his oration at the funeral of activist leader Steve Biko, who died in 1977 of head injuries suffered while in police detention, Tutu urged the crowd to pray for their oppressors in hopes they would realize that non-whites were also human beings, all children of the same God. He related a similar theme at another funeral: "Do not hate. Let us choose the peaceful way to freedom."

In recognition of his ongoing campaign for "truth, freedom, and justice" in South Africa, Tutu received the 1984 Nobel Peace Prize. When presenting the prize, Egil Aarvik, chairman of the Norwegian Nobel Committee, spoke of Tutu's "campaign to solve South Africa's apartheid problem by peaceful means." The contribution Tutu made, Aarvik said, "represents a hope for the future, for the country's white minority as well as the black majority. Desmond Tutu is an exponent of the only form for conflict solving which is worthy of civilized nations."

After receiving the Nobel Peace Prize, Tutu used his monetary award to establish scholarships for promising young South Africans to study in the United States. He was selected as bishop of

Johannesburg and, in 1986, named archbishop of Capetown and metropolitan of the Province of South Africa.

Since then, much has changed within South Africa. Responding in large part to international economic sanctions, South Africa has repealed its apartheid laws. South Africa's foremost political prisoner, Nelson Mandela, even served as the country's president.

The transfer of political power from the minority ruling class to its former subjects has been difficult for both sides. That it occurred without chaos, bloodshed, and civil war is a powerful victory for the non-violent principles propounded so forcefully by Tutu.

In 1995, the Truth and Reconciliation Commission was established by governmental act to officially acknowledge the misdeeds of the apartheid government. Tutu served as its chairman advocating atonement and forgiveness as an essential part of the truth and reconciliation process. He continues to play an important role in his own country and in the world at large as a model of Christian love and temperance.

ARCHBISHOP DESMOND TUTU
"Reconciliation in Post-Apartheid
South Africa: Experiences of the Truth Commission"

I am a preacher. I don't know that you will be exposed to quite the treatment that a particular preacher gave to his congregation: he started preaching, and he went on, and on, and on, and on, and said, at some point, "What more can I say?" And somebody in the back said, "Amen!"

I greet you, dear friends, as someone who comes from what is still described as the "new" South Africa, the "free" South Africa, the "democratic" South Africa, the "non-racial" South Africa, the "non-sexist" South Africa. Almost all of us have described what happened in April 1994, at that historic election, as a miracle, and I think, yes, that is probably the most adequate way of describing something that was almost ineffable. We scored a spectacular victory over the awfulness of apartheid. But you know what? That victory would have been totally impossible without the support that we got from the international community. That victory would have been impossible without the love and the prayers and the commitment of very, very, very many people right around the world. It is not given to too many people who go 'round the world and say, "We have an awful system, please help us to destroy it," and the people give you the help, and the system is destroyed. It is not given to too many to be able to return to those from whom you asked for the support to say, "We've *done* it. *Thank you.*" Thank you, all of you, who made the miracle possible. Thank you. I would like to give you a clap. But it will look weird if I do it all on my own, won't it? So how about joining me in giving you and others who have been part of our support a very, very warm hand.

Thank you, thank you very, very much. I did that once with a group of young people in Australia, and I said, "Part of our trouble is that we don't celebrate who we are. Well, why don't we give ourselves a warm hand," and they did a humdinger of an applause. Then I said, "Let's give God a standing ovation," and they all got up and gave God a standing ovation, and without thinking, I said, "Thank you."

It's been a very great privilege to participate in this colloquium, and very warm congratulations to the University, and to all of those who have been involved, Michele, and Professor Hopkins, and Dean Leffler, and all of those who have been responsible for this splendid initiative. The people sitting around here, my colleagues, you will admit are quite, quite exceptional persons. I am always intrigued by His Holiness particularly, because, you know, he has suffered a great deal. He is in exile from his country for I don't know how many donkey's years, and yet, he has this incredible serenity and bubbliness, joyousness—I was going to say "naughty"—and the world recognizes it.

We speak of a world that is often dismissed as cynical, hard-nosed, and yet actually it has an instinct for goodness. You admire a Nelson Mandela, you admire a Mother Teresa, you admire a Dalai Lama because inside you, there is something that tells you—it hones in to goodness. We condemn this world so frequently, and perhaps quite rightly, for all the awfulnesses there are in it. Awfulnesses caused by us. Sitting and listening to horrendous stories, as we have done, you can't have any illusions about our capacity for evil—that we, all of us, without exception, have the capacity for the most incredible levels of evil. Ahhh, that is just one side of the story, because, *do you know*, we also have an incredible capacity for goodness, and we shouldn't forget that. We shouldn't forget that we have had young people go away from this country, as part of the Peace Corps, go and work in remote places, when they needn't do so and they don't get banner headlines. Young people get banner headlines because they are substance abusers. We forget that actually it was young people, largely, when we were asking, "*Please*, we want sanctions against South Africa." It was young people at universities and colleges who were striving for disinvestment, and I take my hat off to them! Yes, this world has got many awful things, but it also has some very beautiful things. The awful things are that there is a lot of conflict and most of the conflict these days is within nations, within states—it is civil war. Bosnia. Kosovo. Burundi. Rwanda. Sri Lanka. Burma. East Timor. All of these places have a conflict which is going to have to be dealt with.

And how do you deal with a post-conflict, post-repression period, as most of these countries are going to have to do? One way is almost atavistic: revenge. You clobbered mè, I am waiting for my chance to clobber you back. That's exactly what happened in Rwanda. The Hutu did something to the Tutsi, and the Tutsi disappeared for thirty years. They came back, and we had *genocide*. Kosovo. Bosnia. What's happening? Why? Now that's one way.

Another way is the Nuremberg option. Most people say, "Yeah, that probably is not a bad option," but Nuremberg happened where there were clear victors on one side and clear losers on the other side. The winners could enforce, as they say, victors' justice. But have you noticed, in Nuremberg, the prosecutors and the judges, when the trial finished, could pack their cases and leave? In most of the situations we are talking about, the judges, the prosecutors, the perpetrators, and the victims can't up and leave. They have to share the same geographic space. They're going to have to work out: "Hey, how do we, in fact, live together?"

A third option is do nothing. You say, "Let bygones be bygones, let's forget the past. For goodness sake, let's forget the past. Why, why, why do you want to rake up the past? Forget the past, and let's get on with the business of living in the present." You can give yourselves, as they did in Chile, "blanket amnesty." Blanket amnesty, which is really amnesia; we try to forget. But mercifully, mercifully, God has created us in a particular kind of way. The past dealt with in a cavalier fashion does not remain the past; it *refuses* to lie down quietly. Bygones don't become bygones just by your say-so. You don't have a fiat and then you say, "Now, bygones, you are gone." They don't go. They *return* inexorably. They will return to haunt you. You remember those quite haunting words in Dachau, the concentration camp museum, at the entrance: "Those Who Forget the Past Are Doomed to Repeat It."

Yes, but there is the South African way, which didn't happen because South Africans were particularly smart—it was forced on them because of the realities of our situation: no one won. The apartheid government didn't win, the liberation movements didn't win. Stalemate. Hey, how are we going to deal with this? And they struck on this compromise. Compromise tends to have bad press, but it's not always a bad thing, because here they said, "O.K., in exchange for truth, you will get amnesty. In exchange for telling us everything you know about what you want to ask amnesty for, you will get freedom. Of course, if you don't, the judicial process will take its course."

To say "Let us forget about it" was unsatisfactory also for another reason. One of them is that you revictimize the victims. You say to the victims, "What happened in your case either didn't happen, or it doesn't matter." You remember Dorfman's "Death and the Maiden": the woman recognizes the voice of the man who tortured and raped her, and she manages to tie him up. She's got a gun, and he still denies, and she is on the verge of killing him. Then, he turns around and admits he did, and she lets him go, because the lie subverted her identity, her integrity.

We found that just in the *telling of the story,* people have experienced a catharsis, a healing. It has been an incredible privilege, sitting there, and listening to people who, by rights, should be consumed by anger, bitterness, and revenge, and you experience their magnanimity, their willingness to forgive. Of course, you know Nelson Mandela; he is our spectacular example of this sort of thing that has happened in that crazy country. It *is* a crazy country. It's an extraordinary country. But it's been made extraordinary by all of you, upholding us, praying for us, sustaining us, supporting us. You might not believe it, but you are a real part of us. I would not be standing here today, had it not been for some extraordinary people like yourselves.

I want to give you one or two examples, and then I will sit down. A white woman is a victim of a hand-grenade attack by one of the liberation movements. A lot of her friends are killed. She ends up having to have open-heart surgery. Eventually she comes to the Truth and Reconciliation Commission to tell her story. She says, "You know, when I came out of hospital, my children had to bathe me, had to clothe me, had to feed me. And I can't walk through the security checkpoint at an airport—I've still got shrapnel inside me—so, all kinds of alarms go off when I walk through." Do you know what she said of this experience that left her in this condition? "It has"—can you credit it?—"enriched my life." She says, "I'd like to meet the perpetrator, I'd like to meet him in a spirit of forgiveness. I would like to forgive him." Which is extraordinary. But then, she goes on to say—can you believe it?—she goes on to say, "I hope he forgives me."

A second example. One of the former homelands, the Ciskei, banned the ANC from its territory, saying it was a no-go area. The ANC answered they were not going to accept this, and so they went on a march, a demonstration, to Bisho, the capital of this homeland. A number of people were killed because the Ciskei defense force came out, shot and killed a number of people, and injured others. We had a hearing on the so-called Bisho Massacre. The first person who came—and the hearing was in a hall *packed* to the roof by people who had either been injured there, or people who had lost loved ones—to testify is the former head of this Ciskei Defense Force, and, I have to say, even I was riled. Not so much by what he said, as by how he said what he said. The tension you could cut with a knife. Then, the next set of witnesses was four officers: three black, one white. The white was the spokesperson, and he says, "Yes, we gave the orders to the troops to open fire." Yah! The temperature just shot up! Then he turned to the audience and said, "Please forgive us. Please receive these three of my colleagues back into the community." Do you know what the audience did? That audience *broke out into deafening applause.* When the noise had subsided, I said, [*whispering*] "Let's keep quiet, because we are in the presence of something holy. Really, we ought to take off our shoes, because we are standing on holy ground." It's been that kind of experience. Some incredible people. Incredible privilege to have been asked to preside over such a process.

The very last example. The ANC exploded a bomb in Pretoria in one of its main streets, called Church Street. They were attacking the headquarters of the South African Air Force. One of the officers was blinded in that attack, a white man. When the ANC operative applied for amnesty—and amnesty is sought in an open hearing—the ANC Operative, Aboobaker Ismail, turned to Neville Clarence and asked for forgiveness, and the two—the one white blind man and the Indian—shook hands. That picture became a kind of icon. It was emblazoned on the front pages of our newspapers and on television. Neville Clarence said, "As we shook hands, it was as if both of us didn't want to let go of the other."

God has been very good to us, and maybe there is something for the world to learn, from both our mistakes and our achievements. I believe that we are going to succeed in the experiment happening in that crazy country. We are going to succeed because God wants us to succeed. That's not because I have a hotline that I know what God is. God wants us to succeed for the sake of God's world, because God wants to be able to point to Bosnia, Northern Ireland, Middle East, Rwanda, and say, "Just look at them; look at them." Who could ever have imagined that South Africa could be an example of anything but the most ghastly situations, and now God wants to say, "Just look at them." Utterly unlikely! But they are a symbol of hope, South Africa, a symbol of hope. God's sense of humor! "Just look at them, look at them, they're not even too bright, you know, because if they had been bright, smart, they wouldn't have held onto apartheid for so long."

You know the story: A South African was upset that America and the Soviet Union were getting all the kudos for the space program, and so he announced that we, in South Africa, were going to launch a spacecraft to the sun. And then people said, "No, no, no, man, you can't be serious. Long before it reaches the sun, it will be burned to cinders." He says, "Oh, you think we South Africans are stupid? No, no, no, man, we will launch it at night."

God is going to be saying, "They had a nightmare called apartheid. It has ended. Your nightmare will end too. They had a problem that the world had described as being intractable. They are solving it." Bosnia. Kosovo. Sierra Leone. Angola. Burundi. Rwanda. You name them. Your problem can't ever be described again as intractable.

Thank you.

(For a full account of his views and work on the Truth and Reconciliation Commission, see Archbishop's Tutu's *No Future Without Forgiveness,* published by Doubleday, 1999.)

Discussion Among the Participants

Bobby Muller: I really respect what you've done with this effort, and I understand a lot of the emotions that you describe. Having had the opportunity myself to go back to my war zone, meet my former enemy, and come to terms with a tremendous amount of emotion based on the commonality of our experience and having shared the pain of war, was something that put us together much more than that which had separated us on the politics around it. So, I can really appreciate the emotions that you are describing having taken place, but there is an aspect of this which I am totally confused about, and it has to do with personal accountability. You draw the line, and you hold people accountable for, let's say minimally, crimes against humanity, for which I don't think there should be any statute of limitations. I don't think that the fact that Pinochet is an eighty-two-year-old guy should exonerate him or let him off the hook for the torture and the murder of as many innocent people as he is responsible for.

The Nuremberg principles of accountability were accepted; we have Geneva Conventions that describe, in great detail, what make up a body known as the Laws of War. At the beginning of this bloody century, 90 percent of the casualties in conflict were military people, but that has transformed, where today 90 percent of the casualties in these conflicts around the world are innocent civilians. All of this body of agreement, known as the Laws of War as codified in those various mechanisms, apparently seems to mean nothing. One could say that they are not laws, they are sort of like recommendations, because if you break a law, you're punished. South Africa's got a lot which makes it unique, but I am sure you support the idea of an international criminal court to try those guilty of crimes against humanity and support the concept of personal accountability. *Laws* are something that I think we've got to look at. Can you help clarify that a little bit?

Archbishop Desmond Tutu: Yes. What we did at home, in fact, is to take very seriously the whole question of impunity. Before we had our own Truth and Reconciliation Commission, in almost every other instance the military granted themselves amnesty, a blanket amnesty, before moving out. In our case, which is unique, we said amnesty is to be granted on the basis of an individual application. That's one.

Two: the conditions for granting amnesty are not just because you come along and say, "I have done such-and-such." Amnesty is not automatic. We received several thousand applications for amnesty. At the last count, as it were, certainly at the time of the printing of our report, only 154 had been granted, with another 2,000 still to be considered. Thus the second condition is, you acknowledge, you accept, you say you are guilty. That's accountability. There is no point in giving amnesty to someone who is innocent, or claims to be innocent. There are people who came, applied for amnesty, and say they were really innocent, at which point the committee said, "We can't give you amnesty if you are innocent. We can give you amnesty only if you are guilty." People have to accept their responsibility for the atrocity they have committed. And so, your worry about accountability and law, the significance of law, the autonomy of the law, is taken into account.

Lurking behind your question is the concept of justice. Now you say, everybody has got to be punished. Your concept of what constitutes justice is retributive justice. That's not the only kind of justice. We believe that there is restorative justice. The application is heard in an open hearing, not behind closed doors; television lights are on the applicant, and, in fact, for quite a number, this probably was the first time that their wives knew that this apparently decent man was actually a member of a death squad. That public appearance constitutes a public humiliation which is, if you are looking for punitiveness, a punishment. But we didn't think that was where we wanted to end. We were looking for healing, and it's probably an African concept of our understanding of penology. What is the purpose of justice? The purpose is ultimately the restoration of a harmony.

Now, at home we are able, actually, to have the luxury of discussing all of these wonderful things, because this compromise was, in fact, made. Had the security forces known that they were going to be in for the high jump, we wouldn't be sitting here. The victims accepted that there was a price that had to be paid, a price for ensuring that the transition happens. But it isn't a price that is out of proportion to the realities of our situation.

Let me just give you an example. I went to Rwanda very soon after the genocide, to the main prison at Kigali. It was chock-a-block full, and some people had actually died of suffocation. I said to the president of that country, "That jail is a disaster waiting to happen. Your history in this country is this kind of thing. You have a top dog and an underdog. Maybe the top dog is Hutu, the underdog is Tutsi. Your history is: underdog seeks to become top dog, and underdog becomes top dog, and there is hell to pay for the erstwhile top dog, for the things that they did to the new top dog when it was the underdog. And then, the situation turns around. Tutsi now becomes top dog, and Hutu—as is happening now—are the underdog. And the game is played again." I was preaching in Kigali, "If retributive justice is your last word in this country, you have had it. You can write off the possibility of ever having a stable Rwanda." Even as we speak now, the Hutu have mostly been the ones that have been arrested. Mostly Hutu have been found guilty, and Hutu have been executed. They are not going to say, "We were found guilty because the evidence indicated that we were guilty." They will say, "We were found guilty because we are Hutu. We were found guilty by Tutsi judges. We are waiting for our chance." I said to them, "My own understanding, for what it is worth, is that your history of the spiral of reprisal provoking a counter-reprisal provoking a counter-reprisal will remain this way. You need something to go beyond that spiral, to break through. You need forgiveness."

Bobby Muller: I don't want to get lost in a discussion about what constitutes justice; I want to come back to the function of law, and why we have it. Part of it is certainly beyond retribution. I don't see that there is a particular sense of satisfaction in taking, let's say, an eighty-two-year-old guy and throwing him in jail, but one of the functions, clearly, of law is deterrence—to establish as an example those that are guilty of those crimes, so that others who may be contemplating whether or not they want to try to get away with that will have in their mind that if they do it, they will pay a similar price. The deterrent aspect, the accountability factor more than retribution, is the issue.

I have spent a lot of time working with Cambodia for a lot of years. Cambodia changed my life more than the war in Vietnam did, because it was a case of genocide. The war in Vietnam was brutal, but the genocide in Cambodia dismantled the society; it was a chill to my soul and it completely changed my life to have some exposure to the degree of horror that was involved. Well, the guy that really drove the show there was Pol Pot, and shortly before Pol Pot died, he was in a public court, given a chance to explain himself. He said, "Yes, in fact, I'm sorry, I made mistakes."

He may have said that very sincerely—he may have felt, "I made mistakes, but I tried." Where something like that fits in the equation, I think, is open for discussion.

One of the things we talked about earlier today was evil, and how vulnerable we are—as you yourself just said a little while ago—to being seduced by the negative force. We are. We are shockingly vulnerable to being affected. Not that it's quite the same thing, but there was a movie about the marines that Stanley Kubrick put out called *Full Metal Jacket* that illustrates extraordinarily well how eighteen-year-old kids coming into the Marine Corps as basic numbies can be processed, through indoctrination, to wind up charging enemy machine gun positions, which is not a natural act. The point is that there are people—Milosevic, Kabila—who foster the negative and have blood on their hands in a way that demands accountability.

Archbishop Desmond Tutu: Yes. Yes. Perhaps fairly straightforwardly: what we are seeking to do at home is to cultivate a culture of respect for law. We are saying, "You have to take responsibility for what you did." You have to stand up in an open forum and say, "I have done so-and-so." Remember, the amnesty provision is not something that is going to stay on forever; it's a provision for a transition. There is a limitation to when a person can apply for amnesty. In our case, it is long over. That is why part of our recommendation is, for those who did not apply for amnesty—and where there is evidence that they were guilty of violations, gross violations, of human rights—that the judicial process should take its course.

I think that, even with the amnesty process, it incorporates your deterrence element. No one wants to stand up in public and say, "I abducted this young man. I gave him spiked coffee, and I shot him in the head. I burned his body, and whilst we were burning his body, we had a barbecue." Which is something that was part of the testimony in one case—I mean, nobody likes being known in public in that kind of way. So there is a deterrent. The very fact that not everybody applied shows that there is a reluctance to appear. But with regard to Pol Pot, the fact that he stands up and says, "I am sorry, I made mistakes," unless the country says that they are willing to have an amnesty provision, I don't think that that is, actually, a relevant example for the kind of thing that I am trying to talk about. I am talking about a specific situation—and we're going to get many such situations of transition. It's going to happen in East Timor. They are going to try to work it out: "We had collaborators with the Indonesians; how are we going to deal with them?" They can't just say, "Well, it's O.K., we will forget about it," because they won't forget about it! They've got to find a mechanism. We are not claiming that this is an infallible blueprint; it is an option that people ought to be considering as a serious option.

Dr. Rigoberta Menchú Tum: I think that this topic is of tremendous importance. The Nobel Laureates, and perhaps other institutions, should put together a program of study, a program of work, to trace a line of work to produce a systematic gathering of the experiences of amnesties, and also the experiences of truth and justice in areas of conflict. I, as a victim, would like to identify those responsible for the torture and death of my mother. If I were to find them, I would like to bring them before justice and for them at least to demonstrate their innocence of all these things. On behalf of the victims, there can be decrees, but the solution of damage that has been done is not a matter of a decree. How can we hope that they at least ask for forgiveness? I can't forget that forgiveness comes with truth and with justice, and thus I recognize Bobby's concern—what can we do to perfect the process by which we address this in the future? The past is something that we lived, that we have acted in. Often, the processes of peace have ended in a climate of impunity, but how, in the future, can we make it so that impunity does not have a place in the countries that have suffered these conflicts?

Julian Bond: Your Grace, before you answer that question, I want to see if Harn Yawnghwe and Betty Williams also have opinions on this.

Harn Yawnghwe: I am very interested because we have a very brutal regime in Burma and we will have to come to terms with it soon. Both your experience, and maybe José's in East Timor, and maybe in Guatemala, you have this basic concept—either Catholic or Protestant—of forgiveness. Will it work in a situation like Burma where, really, we don't have a concept of forgiveness? We have compassion, we may excuse people, but the concept of forgiveness is something quite different. I know there is not enough time, but that's something I really would like to explore.

Betty Williams: Dear, dear, dear Father Tutu. I love you so much, because the only way forward for the world is in forgiveness, and I think that South Africa has created a model that should be copied by other places. Burma could learn a lot from His Grace's work in South Africa. One of the things that bothers me is this question of law, and when the law, as we know, has no respect for the people, then the people will have no respect for the law. I taught in Texas for four years at a university, and while I was there, the then-governor, Ann Richards, appointed me to the Texas Commission of Children and Youth. The answer to everything in Texas was to build bigger and better prisons. And I mean, "Duh! Don't you know that if you work in the ghetto, you won't need the prison to be as big?" We spend billions and billions of dollars here in the United States of America incarcerating people instead of spending the same billions of dollars in the ghettoes for better housing, jobs for people, and all of that. It just doesn't make sense.

Julian Bond: Your Grace, can you summarize?

Archbishop Desmond Tutu: I concur with Betty. I don't know about Buddhists not knowing anything about forgiveness. What happens when you quarrel with your wife?

Harn Yawnghwe: I don't!

Archbishop Desmond Tutu: In every language, every culture, the most difficult words you have to say are, "I'm sorry. Forgive me." Otherwise, actually, there is no future in that relationship. Basically, I am saying that even in the world, forgiveness is not just a spiritual something that is nebulous. It is in fact realpolitik: there will be no future without forgiveness. That is for real. Consider this military junta in Burma that is scared of a woman who is about that size [*holds one hand above the other a few inches apart*] speaking about authority, moral authority. Our sister laureate is remarkable in her gentleness and her willingness to say, "Let's talk." That is maybe the paradigm that the world wants to be looking at.

Questions from the Audience

Jeffrey Hopkins: This is a question for President Arias. The notions of human rights and reconciliation of conflicts seem to appeal to and invoke a common bond that exists among all beings. What is that common bond, and why is it so frequently forgotten?

President Oscar Arias Sánchez: The common bond is common values, isn't it? Common moral values. The ones that have been mentioned here: tolerance, the force of dialogue, of understanding. What we have been talking about this afternoon: forgiveness. I think that what makes social togetherness viable are common values.

Jeffrey Hopkins: Then, for Betty Williams. How can one strike a balance in daily life between forgiveness and standing up for oneself?

Betty Williams: Oh dear. I am not known to be very even-tempered. I can forgive very easily; it's the forgetting I have a problem with. Much to my shame, Your Grace. Because every now and again, I think, "Well that person did so-and-so," and that little devil imp gets on this shoulder, and for a while forgiveness goes out the window. Standing up for oneself, I guess, depends on what one's self wants. What are you standing up for? I stand up for children. What does standing up mean? I'm like His Holiness on this one: I don't know.

Jeffrey Hopkins: Then, a question for Harn Yawnghwe. Why isn't Aung San Suu Kyi present here?

Harn Yawnghwe: She's not present here because she really can't be. Let me try to explain. The military would very much like her to get out of the country because by being in the country, she is creating a lot of problems for them and thus they would love to see her leave Burma. But if she were to get on a plane and go somewhere, anywhere, they would never let her back in. That is the reason she is not here.

Jeffrey Hopkins: Thank you for representing her here. This is a question for Jody Williams. Would you comment on Amnesty International's decision to add the United States to its list of countries guilty of serious human rights violations.

Jody Williams: Given their history of solid documentation of abuses of human rights, if they have added the United States to the list, I assume it should be there.

Jeffrey Hopkins: This is a question for Dr. Menchú Tum. In light of the enormous tragedies you have suffered in your fight for peace and justice, what gives you the strength to carry on?

Dr. Rigoberta Menchú Tum: I have always thought that when one lives through something, one must live through that thing. We have no alternative but to do so. People who are victims have had no alternative but to live the experiences that they live. The hope that one has that the world will one day be different is that no one will have to live through the things that one has experienced. This becomes a profound conviction—that human beings must find a way to live with each other, a way to live together. I also gain strength from people, from women and from those people who work in little corners that go unrecognized, but sure of a new future. I have seen that when people obtain something—a school, or something like this—this gives them the energy to keep on going. Every success makes them live life anew. So, I believe that we have no reason to complain about history, about our history; what gives people the strength to carry on are our mutual interests and the possibilities for the future. Above all, we Maya believe that all of us are but passers-by on this earth, that we are here for a short time, and that we must do something while we pass through. This is what motivates me.

Jeffrey Hopkins: And a final question for Archbishop Tutu. Based on your experience of sanctions toward South Africa, what do you think about the current U.S. sanctions on Burma?

Archbishop Desmond Tutu: In South Africa, we would not have succeeded quite to the extent that we did, and perhaps with so much less bloodshed than would otherwise have been the case, had it not been for the sanctions. We have said, as laureates, when we went to Thailand on behalf of our sister laureate, Aung San Suu Kyi, that we were calling on Western countries, and Asian countries, to notice that this is a non-violent strategy for changing an unjust system. We went also to the White House and made the same plea. We have to say that President Clinton was very good to have responded positively to our particular plea.

You get all sorts of people saying all sorts of things about sanctions: that they will hurt the people you are trying to help. Twiddle! It's baloney of the first order! Because you are speaking about people already suffering, and you are saying you are trying to find some way that is a non-violent strategy for bringing about the change that everybody says they want. We would—well let me say that I haven't consulted my colleagues—I would want to say as firmly as I can that it is a moral issue. It's asking: are you on the side of right or the side of wrong? Are you on the side of justice, or on the side of injustice? Are you on the side of freedom or oppression? It is very clear. Everything else is obfuscating, and I would be pleased that we do all we can to put the screws on that military junta, that they should accept the result of the election.

I know you were saying that this is the last question, wasn't it?

Jeffrey Hopkins: Yes.

Archbishop Desmond Tutu: But may I just have a last word? The God that I worship is a strange God, because it is God who is omnipotent, all-powerful, but He is also God who is weak. An extraordinary paradox: that it is God, a God of justice, who wants to see justice in the world, but because God has such a deep reverence for our freedoms all over the place, God will not intervene, like sending lightning bolts to dispatch all despots. God waits for God's partners: us. God has a dream. God has a dream of a world that is different, a world in which you and I care for one another because we belong in one family. I want to make an appeal on behalf of God. God says, "Can you help me realize my dream? My dream of a world that is more caring, a world that is more compassionate, a world that says people matter more than things. People matter more than profits. That is my dream," says God. "Will you please help me realize my dream? I have nobody, except you."

President Oscar Arias Sánchez

Costa Rica

Short Biography

"Peace is a process which never ends," Oscar Arias Sánchez once said. "It is the result of innumerable decisions made by many persons in many lands. It is an attitude, a way of life, a way of solving problems and of resolving conflicts. It cannot be forced on the smallest nation, nor can it be imposed by the largest. It can neither ignore our differences nor overlook our common interests. It requires us to work and live together."

Arias speaks from experience. As the man who helped bring peace to a conflict-ridden Central America, he has earned the respect of many for his consensus-building ability.

By the time Arias became president of Costa Rica in 1986, Central America had experienced great regional turmoil for many years. Government armies and civilian guerrilla groups in El Salvador, Guatemala, and Nicaragua were waging wars that had led to the exile, torture, imprisonment, and death of countless people.

In Nicaragua, the strife was exacerbated by military intervention from the United States and Soviet Union. The United States was organizing and supplying antigovernment rebels known as Contras, while the Soviet Union and Cuba were aiding the Marxist Sandinista government. This intervention only aggravated the internal unrest in Guatemala and El Salvador and increased border tensions between Nicaragua and its neighbors, Honduras and Costa Rica—both of which had tried to remain neutral. Because of security concerns and dependence on aid from the United States, they eventually capitulated to outside pressure: Honduras permitted the construction of Contra military bases, while Costa Rica let the United States construct a secret airport for transporting supplies to the Contras.

Concerned about these and other events, leaders in Mexico, Venezuela, Colombia, and Panama drafted the Contadora peace plan for Central America in 1983. Unfortunately, despite initial support from the five Central American countries it was intended to help, fundamental differences in interpreting the plan kept it from succeeding.

Oscar Arias Sánchez was one of many who were disappointed by the Contadora plan's failure. A native of Costa Rica, he was a champion of democratic and peaceful values. He had first-hand knowledge of American democracy, gained while briefly attending Boston University in the United States. At that time, John F. Kennedy and Richard Nixon were vying for the American presidency, and Arias followed the contest closely. Kennedy would later become one of Arias' political role models.

After returning to his homeland, Arias earned degrees in law and economics from the University of Costa Rica in 1967. Next, he attended the University of Essex, England. In 1969, he returned from England to teach political science at the University of Costa Rica and continue his research for his doctoral dissertation, a socio-economic analysis of Costa Rican political leadership. He published his first book, *Grupos de Presión en Costa Rica* (*Pressure Groups in Costa Rica*) in 1970, which received the 1971 National Essay Prize. The University of Essex awarded him a Ph.D. in 1974.

His expertise in economics captured the attention of José Figueres Ferrer, the country's former liberal president who had abolished the Costa Rican army in 1948 and who was returning to the presidency after a twelve-year absence. Figueres appointed Arias to his economic council in 1970 and, two years later, named Arias as his minister of national planning and economic policy. The full-time cabinet post forced Arias to resign from teaching, although he has remained committed to the country's free and compulsory educational system.

Arias retained his cabinet post until 1978, when he was elected to the Costa Rican Congress as a representative of the National Liberation Party. In 1981, he became the party's secretary-general, and in 1986 he was elected president of his nation.

Achieving peace in Central America became one of his greatest priorities. Soon after taking presidential office, he closed down the secret U.S. airbase and met with four Central American leaders to see whether the Contadora peace plan could be revived.

Based on their discussions, in February 1987 Arias presented a new peace plan. The "Procedure for the Establishment of a Firm and Lasting Peace in Central America" called for the creation of a national reconciliation commission that would oversee amnesty for all guerrilla soldiers, a concurrent cease fire, the right to freedom of expression and democratic elections, and the release of political prisoners. It also stipulated the cessation of all military aid from or to outside governments—whether that aid be in the form of money, supplies, or the use of Central American territories for military purposes. Five Central American presidents signed the accord in Guatemala on August 27, 1987.

These efforts earned Arias, at age forty-six, the 1987 Nobel Peace Prize. In presenting the award, Egil Aarvik, Norwegian Nobel Committee chairman, acknowledged that Arias was not working in isolation. "The fact that the plan is the result of a cooperation between the five signatory states indicates that there is in fact a general recognition that the time is ripe," he said. "The peace prize to Oscar Arias is therefore to be interpreted as a recognition also of the work of the other heads of state and their work with the plan."

A year after receiving the prize, Arias established the Arias Foundation for Peace and Human Progress, a non-profit organization dedicated to building "just and peaceful societies in Central America." The foundation's three programmatic areas have worked diligently to promote gender equality, strengthen "the participation and action of civil society," and resolve military conflicts in the developing world.

His efforts on behalf of human development, democracy, and demilitarization have earned Arias honorary doctorate degrees from Harvard, Dartmouth, and other universities and colleges. He has also received further prizes, including the Martin Luther King Jr. Peace Award and the Albert Schweitzer Humanitarian Award.

In response to his growing concern about global arms trading, in 1995 Arias invited fellow Nobel Peace Laureates to join him in developing an International Code of Conduct on Arms Transfers. The code, which was jointly signed by eight Peace Laureates on May 29, 1997, in New York City, governs all arms transfers, including conventional weapons and munitions, military and security training, and sensitive military and dual-use technologies. It stipulates that a country wishing to purchase arms must promote democracy, protect human rights, and be open about its military spending. It also prohibits arms sales to nations that support terrorism and to states engaged in aggression toward other nations or peoples.

PRESIDENT OSCAR ARIAS SÁNCHEZ
"International Code of Conduct on Arms Transfers"

What an honor it is to be in the presence of my fellow Nobel Peace Laureates and to be able to share ideas with such a distinguished audience of students, educators, and activists. Truly, I thank Jeffrey Hopkins, Daniel Ehnbom, Michele Bohana, and Bryan

Phillips for inviting me to speak today, and I extend my gratitude to all of those who have worked to organize this conference.

I have been asked to speak with you about the idea of an international code of conduct on arms transfers, but first, I must set this discussion within the larger context of the struggle for human security that we face at the present moment. I am sure that you have seen many times the images of the Berlin Wall coming down, watched commentators pronounce the end of the Cold War, and heard that a new era has begun. Indeed, few terms are as important today as "globalization." Though only a small number of individuals take time to closely examine this concept, many feel entitled to invoke it regularly. Not only does globalization portend to characterize our present age, but it also seems to carry the weight of destiny. Certainly, technological advances and the emergence of sophisticated markets have increased the affinity between different global societies, allowing for rapid transportation of people and information.

But globalization points to several other distinctive phenomena as well. Traditional understandings of economies, and traditional understandings of economics, are changing. For some, the new economic system means being able to make investments with a worldly perspective, minimizing labor costs and maximizing profits. For many others, it means facing the end of job security and at the same time witnessing the reappearance of sweatshops. Structures of governments also adapt to a new world order. Conventionally, states find themselves weakened in the face of transnational agreements and fluid capital. The $1.5 trillion that race around the planet daily are largely unaccountable to any accepted form of public oversight.

This globalization is a Janus-faced beast, offering unimaginable prosperity to the most well-educated and well-born, while doling out only misery and despair to the world's poor. The system encourages insatiable consumption for some but denies many others the basic necessities of life. Who would not question the priorities of a system in which Americans spend eight billion dollars a year on cosmetics, two billion more than it would cost to provide basic education for everyone in the world, if these funds were redirected. Europeans spend eleven billion dollars a year purchasing ice cream, yet we know that only nine billion dollars a year would be adequate to assure water and sanitation for all people.

While in past years the dissenting viewpoints on globalization had been muted, today things have changed. Undoubtedly, you are all aware that we are in the midst of a global financial crisis. Now, we can watch even the high priests of the unregulated market, powerless in preventing panic, coming down from their pulpits. Rather than sanctifying the capricious benevolence of the invisible hand, many are falling to their knees and hoping that total collapse will be averted. Jeffrey Sachs, the Harvard economist who supervised the program of "shock therapy" for Russia and much of Eastern Europe, now tells us that the "dream of quick economic liberalization lies in ruins."

But, what is not stressed in the talk of Wall Street analysts, who seem preoccupied with the profitability of their investment houses, is the true human dimension of this crisis. Imagine if half of the people you know—people earning a modest but adequate living—were suddenly thrown into desperate poverty. This is the situation that our brothers and sisters in Indonesia are now confronting, as 100 million people are made to feel the crushing blow of financial panic. The economies of Thailand and South Korea have shrunk by 45 percent in the past two years; indeed, the currency of South Korea lost half of its value in the past year, witnessing substantial declines in a matter of days. And as the shock waves from this devaluation extend through society, it is the most vulnerable and economically insecure populations who often bear the miserable brunt of the impact. These people do not need a market observer to tell them of the shortcomings of an economic system based on greed and speculation, rather than on human need.

Moreover, compassionate people can only shudder when they consider the combined horrors of military insecurity and human desperation in Russia. Every day we receive word that the safeguards protecting the country's twenty-two thousand nuclear weapons are growing less secure. Even before the turmoil of the past few months, life expectancy for males declined from a pre-reform 65.6 years to 57 years today, a decline unheard of in times without war or massive natural disaster. And, as winter begins, there are indications that millions of people may die, lacking food to strengthen their bodies and fuel to warm their homes, unless the international community undertakes a massive humanitarian intervention, and not merely a bail-out for wealthy investors.

Thus, while the age of the Cold War has ended, it has not been followed by the promised era of peace and prosperity. For how can we say that there is peace when thousands are made to work under dehumanizing conditions? How can we say that there is peace when the United States builds more prisons and fewer schools? How can we say that there is peace when so many go hungry?

This historical moment requires that we think about peace in a new way. Traditionally, peace has been discussed with reference to the demands of national security. The United Nations Development Program, however, stresses the need for us, instead, to think of peace in terms of human security. This distinction bears frequent repetition. Human security goes beyond concern with weapons—it is a concern with human life and dignity. When we demand peace, it must be not only a peace which holds back bombing and gunfire. It must also be a peace concerned with the welfare and health of all people. For truly, when poverty and inequality remain at such terrible levels, armed conflict will be inevitable.

During the Great Depression of the 1930s, Franklin D. Roosevelt looked out on 40 million people "ill-housed, ill-clad, ill-fed." Now, with our global vision, we must face over thirty times as many fellow citizens living in desperate circumstances. Each person must face the fact that of the 4.4 billion people living in the developing world, nearly three-fifths lack access to adequate sewers; a third have no access to clean water; a quarter live in woefully sub-standard housing; and a fifth have no access to modern health services of any kind. As a result, forty thousand children die each day from malnutrition and disease, and nearly one-third of the people in the least developed countries are not expected to survive to the age of forty. While the world, as a whole, consumes twenty-four trillion dollars worth of goods and services each year, the planet holds 1.3 billion people who live on incomes of less than one dollar a day.

In human history, our societies have always known poverty and suffering. But what makes the poverty of today so sinister is that this terrible suffering exists alongside tremendous wealth. Today, the three richest people in the world have assets that exceed the combined gross domestic product of the poorest forty-eight countries. In the United States, the richest 20 percent earn nine times more than the poorest 20 percent; this country has one of the worst distributions of wealth in a world full of stark inequalities. Indeed, my friends, our global society cannot sustain these inequalities. Decent people, concerned with peace and justice, cannot allow them to persist.

It is a great disappointment to me that we have so few leaders willing to stand up to the evils of poverty and inequality. Despite the huge potentials for moral progress in the current age, the ethics of greed and militarism remain. Beneath all the talk of presidential embarrassment and cover-up, lies an even deeper and more disgraceful scandal, one that few leaders have the courage to address. The true scandal is that rather than proudly pronouncing the end of world poverty, so many policy makers and business people are solidifying a global economic order based on cynicism and individual property. The true scandal is that rather than promoting the noble values of compassion and solidarity, leaders quietly allow the most wealthy to prosper at the expense of poor and working people throughout the world. The true scandal is that politicians tell the people what they want to hear instead of what they need to know.

Sadly, these same politicians underestimate the impact that suffering in the inner cities and tragic poverty in the wider world have on the democratic consciousness, disheartening all those who dream of a more just, humane society. Thus, those here may have little trouble relating to the words of Robert Kennedy, a graduate of this great university, who told us:

> While each of us may not be poor, poverty affects *all* of us.... The facts of poverty and injustice penetrate to every corner, every suburb and every farm in this nation.... Our ideal of America is a nation in which justice is done. And, therefore, the continued existence of injustice—of unnecessary and inexcusable poverty in this most favored of nations—this knowledge erodes our ideal of America, our basic sense of who and what we are. It is, in the deepest sense of the word, demoralizing to all of us.

The lack of moral leadership will only be rectified if global citizens demand a new ethics for the new millennium. When Voltaire wrote *Candide* over two hundred years ago, he was acutely aware of the moral obligations created by an integrating world. In this book, Candide meets a slave from the Americas who is missing both a hand and a leg. The slave's hand was cut off by dangerous machinery in a sugarcane mill; his leg was cut off by cruel masters to prevent him from escaping. As Candide looks on, the miserable slave tells him, "This is the true price of the sugar you eat in Europe."

If ethics required global thinking in Voltaire's time, think of how relevant this powerful anecdote is in the age of globalization.

As Americans today, you have only to look at the label on your clothes and wonder if foreign garment workers labored for a just wage to see that you already participate in the global system that brings great wealth to some and great misery to many others. The question is not whether you will be involved in the ethical challenges of globalization, but what your contribution will be. Will you, in your apathy, be complicit in the injustices I have described? Or will you, with your action and your example, bolster the ranks of those fighting for human security?

The age of narrow-minded nationalism has ended. Today, we must accept the fact that the evils of environmental destruction and human deprivation, of disease and malnutrition, of conspicuous consumption and military build-up, are global problems—problems which affect us all. Each of you must reconsider the privilege you enjoy as well-educated citizens in a wealthy country, and you must embrace the responsibility that comes with this privilege. The point is not to feel guilty about the gifts you have received, but to feel always committed to the struggle to guarantee that all people may live such dignified lives. Do not be overwhelmed by the problems we face. Instead, be determined to make your mark against poverty and inequality, for it is this determination that builds hope, and it is hope that allows people to join together in the movements that change the world.

Do not doubt that such movements have accomplished much. The United Nations Development Program reports that in the past fifty years, poverty has fallen more than in the previous five hundred. Infant mortality in the developing world is one-third what it was in 1960. And during this same period of time, life expectancy in the poorest countries has been extended more than fifteen years, owing largely to a revolution in women's health.

I share these facts with you not so that we may grow complacent and stop working, but to convey a sense of the momentous possibilities for progress. Did it not take a movement of scorned but persistent abolitionists to end the scourge of slavery? Let us similarly join together today to end the scourge of poverty. Did not relentless advocates for independence succeed in ending colonialism? Let us now join in solidarity with the oppressed people of the world so that all may know freedom and liberty.

The United States often stresses the rosy fictions of general prosperity, but too often fails to take responsibility for its role in sustaining injustice. In his recent address to the Russian people, President Clinton argued that the countries of the world should, I quote, "harness the genius of our citizens not for making weapons, but for building better communications, curing disease, combating hunger, and exploring the heavens." Unfortunately, one can only wonder if these optimistic words do not themselves express a certain cynicism. President Clinton speaks to the benefits of disarmament while U.S. missiles fly over Sudan and while the U.S. government assures the Pentagon billions of dollars more than it asked for. Many people in the U.S. government, and even many people within the Clinton Administration, have spoken in theory to the benefits of demilitarization, but commit themselves in practice to the sale of deadly armaments.

Since the end of the Cold War, many industrialized nations have reduced their defense budgets. As a result, those countries' arms merchants have turned to new clients in the developing world, where the majority of today's conflicts take place. The United States stands out as an extreme case. Currently, the U.S. is responsible for 44 percent of all weapons sales in the world, and between 1993 and 1996, 85 percent of U.S. arms sales to the developing world went to non-democratic governments.

At the end of 1997, weapons manufactured in the United States were being used in thirty-nine of the world's forty-two ethnic and territorial conflicts. It is unconscionable for a country that believes in democracy and justice to continue allowing arms merchants to reap profits stained in blood. But, ironically, vast amounts of taxpayer money go to support this immoral trade. In 1995, the arms industry received $7.6 billion in federal subsidies—this amounts to a huge welfare payment to wealthy profiteers.

In order to understand the true human costs of militarism, as well as the true impact of unregulated arms sales in the world today, we must understand that war is not just an evil act of destruction—it is a missed opportunity for humanitarian investment. It is a crime against every child who calls out for food rather than for guns, and against every mother who demands simple vaccinations rather than million-dollar fighters. Without a doubt, military spending represents the single most significant perversion of global priorities known today, claiming $780 billion in 1997. If we channeled just 5 percent of that figure over the next ten years into anti-poverty programs, all of the world's population would enjoy basic social services. Another 5 percent, or $40 billion, over ten years would provide all people on this planet with an income above the poverty line for their country.

Unfortunately, half of the world's governments dedicate more resources to defense than to health programs. Such distortions in national budgets contribute to poverty and retard human development. War, and the preparation for war, is one of the greatest obstacles to human progress, fostering a vicious cycle of arms build-ups, violence, and poverty.

Examples abound throughout the world of instances where arms purchases have resulted in suffering and injustice. Perhaps one of the most relevant comes from South Asia, where an arms race rages between India and Pakistan, fueled by the dispute over the Kashmir Territory. India has spent more than twelve billion dollars on arms purchases from 1988 to 1992 alone—more than either Saudi Arabia or Iraq during that same period. From 1978 to 1991, Pakistan increased its defense budget sevenfold, so that defense now accounts for nearly 40 percent of all government spending. More recently, these countries have raised the horrible specter of nuclear war with highly publicized atomic testing. We can only hope that courageous and dissenting voices in these countries will further propel Pakistan's and India's leaders toward endorsing the Comprehensive Test Ban Treaty, an agreement that has yet to be ratified by the U.S. Congress.

From regional conflicts and terrorist strikes, we have learned that aggressively exporting deadly weaponry not only hurts the poor of the world, but also comes back to endanger even the citizens of developed countries. When will lawmakers learn that when we allow arms merchants to profit in death, no one is safe?

For over a year now, my friends, I have worked to advocate an International Code of Conduct on Arms Transfers, a comprehensive, international effort to regulate and monitor weapons sales. This agreement demands that any decision to export arms should take into account several characteristics pertaining to the country of final destination. The recipient country must endorse democracy, defined in terms of free and fair elections, the rule of law, and civilian control over the military and security forces. Its government must not engage in gross violations of internationally recognized human rights. The International Code of Conduct would not permit arms sales to any country engaged in armed aggression in violation of international law.

Many say that such a code is impractical—impractical because it puts concern for human life before a free market drive for profits; impractical because it listens to the poor who are crying out for schools and doctors, rather than the dictators who demand guns and fighters. Yes, in an age of cynicism and greed, all just ideas are considered impractical. You are discouraged if you say that we can live in peace. You are mocked for insisting that we can be more humane.

But I am proud to say that I am not alone in denouncing this cowardly status quo and in supporting an International Code of Conduct on Arms Transfers. Indeed, today I am in good company to promote this ambitious agreement. For, Nobel Peace

Laureates Elie Wiesel, Betty Williams, and the Dalai Lama stood with me in presenting the code last year. So did José Ramos-Horta, Amnesty International, the American Friends Service Committee, and the International Physicians for the Prevention of Nuclear War. Since then, Archbishop Desmond Tutu and Rigoberta Menchú have joined this impractical group, as have Lech Walesa, Adolfo Perez Esquivel, Mairead Maguire, Norman Borlaug, Joseph Rotblat, and Jody Williams. In all, seventeen winners of the Nobel Peace Prize, as well as former President Jimmy Carter, have endorsed the code. But more importantly, thousands of individuals, groups, and community leaders have expressed their belief that a code of conduct is not only a morally sound idea, but also a politically necessary agreement. It is these people, and the force of their convictions, that turn possibility into progress and turn practical ideas into reality.

Though much work remains, the code effort has made genuine progress. On May 25th of this year, European Union foreign ministers agreed to the terms of Europe's first Code of Conduct on Arms Exports, which now remains to be implemented on its strength and in various key areas. Across the Atlantic here in the United States, owing to back-room dealings, a U.S. Code of Conduct on Arms Transfers has failed to pass a joint House-Senate Conference Committee. Nevertheless, advocates have continued to fight for U.S. legislation that would generally limit the arms trade, even as they have forced the weapons industry to propose a deceptive and irresponsible version of the code.

President Clinton has recently announced that fighting terrorism will be a key priority in U.S. foreign policy. If the President, and indeed all national leaders, are serious about stemming international terror, they must look first at their own policy of arms sales to undemocratic governments worldwide. Moreover, they must actively support the International Code of Conduct as a means of reducing the global availability of deadly weapons. In the federal government, some courageous representatives have stepped forward to champion the code effort. Unfortunately, we cannot expect all national lawmakers, many of whom have received large campaign donations from arms merchants, to stand up to the weapons industry on their own. Congress as a whole will not respond to the moral demands of the code unless those here today, and many, many others like you, generate the kind of popular pressure that forces immediate action.

Friends, you will remember that at the beginning of my remarks, I addressed the unique challenges to human security that our complex and changing world presents. Truly, no one can deny that a new era of globalization has begun. But I can say with equal certainty that this new era has not ended—its final force and significance have yet to be determined. Globalization, if skillfully managed, can be, indeed, a great opportunity. It can be a promising chance for progress in the developing world. But we must remember that unregulated markets are not divine or uncontrollable creatures; they are human creations, subject to moral oversight and intervention. Those working today can decide whether the age of globalization will be remembered as a time of profit and plunder, or as a time of diversity and enlightenment. All of you here will decide, with your activism or your complacency, whether the new world order will be governed by corporate ethics of selfishness or by an ethical charter of equality and human rights.

In conclusion, I want to stress that although the International Code of Conduct on Arms Transfers would be a significant step in promoting global security and protecting human rights, it is not an end in itself. For, the struggle for human security will not end until the world undertakes a comprehensive and humanitarian demilitarization. It will not end until all people enjoy fundamental liberties. And it will not end until all public policy embodies a thoroughgoing affirmation of human dignity.

I am but one person in a larger *movement*. It is a movement of many people in many walks of life, all working to see that these just ends are realized. Together, we gather our courage and our determination; for when we do *not* lack these, we will embark on a great journey. Our path will be perilous, but our eminent destination will be a new, more humane planet Earth. Many of my fellow laureates, and many of the scholars and activists in this audience, have already helped to lead us on our odyssey. To all of the rest of you, I say that the moral journey to a better world is a trip worth taking, *and I invite you to join us.*

Thank you.

Discussion Among the Participants

Julian Bond: Yesterday, Mr. President, you said you were a supporter of the market system, and indeed the market system in the great struggle of the Cold War has triumphed. Yet, it is as unforgiving, quite often, as the corporate ethics you spoke about just a moment ago. How are we to balance the unforgiving nature of the market system with the very real demands of the poor?

President Oscar Arias Sánchez: I believe, Professor Bond, that everybody agrees now that with globalization of the market system, of communications, of capital flows, etc., some people will become losers and some winners. Certainly, those who have no education or little education will be losers. Those who have a good education will be the winners. So, it's very simple: How can we spend, like in many countries in Africa and the Middle East and in Asia, three times more of GDP on defense, on huge armies which are not needed, on forces which very often are used simply to oppress the people or other people—like Indonesia or Turkey or Iraq—instead of educating our children?

To govern is to educate. A statesman is that person who tells people what people need to know. A politician is that person who tells people what people want to hear. We need to educate the leaders of today, so that they have the courage and determination to tell people what people need to know. What the children in Latin America, in Asia, and in Africa need is schools and health clinics, and not F-16s and tanks.

Betty Williams: Mr. President, congratulations for the work you already achieved. I would like you, if you would, to tell the audience how you managed to disarm two countries.

President Oscar Arias Sánchez: I believe everybody would agree that it's more important, much more important, to convince, to persuade, than to conquer. That's the essence of leadership, after all. When Noriega was ousted in December of 1989, a new president was sworn in in the Panama Canal Zone. His name was Guillermo Endara, and because he became president as a result of an invasion, no Latin American country wanted to recognize the new government in Panama. So, when I went to Panama City to meet President Endara, I told him, "Since I am your neighbor to the north and since I will be leaving office very soon, I would like to recognize your government under one condition: if you get rid of the armed forces." That's called "Costa Rican imperialism"! And he said to me, "Well, let me think it over." So I raised some funds to initiate a campaign in Panama to persuade the people that it was a good idea, because, according to the Panamanian Constitution, in order to amend the Constitution, a referendum is needed. To make a long story short, I was able to persuade the members of Parliament, and the Constitution was amended. As a consequence of that, I tell my friends in Washington that the safest border in the world is that between Costa Rica and Panama.

Again, just before President Aristide was sent back by the Clinton Administration to Haiti, to Port-au-Prince, I again met with President Aristide in Washington, and I told him, "You should go back and finish your term. But, it is even more important for you to go back and get rid of the armed forces." Haiti, as you all know, is the poorest country in this hemisphere. It is a country which became independent in 1803, before any other Latin American country, and the armed forces have been responsible for twenty-six coups d'etat since then. The armed forces are corrupt, like in many Latin American countries or Asia or Africa, and they were the main source of instability for that nation. Again, I raised funding from some enlightened Nordic countries; we initiated a campaign in Haiti, and again we were able to convince the legislators that they should amend the Constitution.

What I want to say is that Costa Rica's case is not unique. It can be replicated in other parts of the world. Only recently, the Arias Foundation held a conference in Arusha, Tanzania, with the defense ministers of sub-Saharan Africa, and I am in the process now of persuading the government of Sierra Leone to get rid of the armed forces. The president of Sierra Leone will be visiting Costa Rica and Panama next February or March, in order to share with us our own experience. What we, in the developing world, need are welfare estates, not garrison estates. To govern is to choose, as we all know—we need to choose between the education of our children or pleasing the military people.

Harn Yawnghwe: If I may ask a somewhat controversial question: You mentioned that three of the richest people in the world have more wealth than the poorest forty-eight nations, and I think it is also true of corporations. Many corporations are bigger than many nations. Do you think we are wasting our time working on governments? Trying to control things, we work with the United Nations, we work with governments, but the actual power base has shifted to the corporations, and in the name of free trade and globalization, there are almost no restrictions on corporations. How can we deal with that? This will be the problem of the future.

President Oscar Arias Sánchez: Yes. I agree with you. We all know that, as I pointed out, capital flow amounts to $1.5 trillion a day.

If you look at foreign direct investment from corporations, it amounts to more than $300 billion a year. Two-thirds of those investments go to the industrialized nations; one-third goes to developing nations. Of this one-third that goes to developing nations, about 85 percent goes to twelve countries, China being the most important one. So, the poorest countries get very little. As a matter of fact, sub-Saharan Africa gets no more than 2 percent of foreign direct investment. A country like Nicaragua, a country like Honduras, a country like Haiti, gets peanuts. A country like Bangladesh gets just a few million dollars. So, we are competing with Russia, we are competing with Eastern Europe, we are competing with Southeast Asia, we are competing with China in order to attract foreign direct investment—to attract corporations to invest in our countries. In order to be able to compete, we need to provide them with some basic infrastructure. How can we build that infrastructure if we are spending 3, 4, and 5 percent of GDP on arms?

It's as simple as that. Demilitarization is not an end in itself. In our discussions yesterday, the word "poverty" was not mentioned. I have mentioned poverty and inequality about ten times today. My main concern, because this is a real danger for peace, is poverty. Poverty needs no passport to travel, and I don't want this great nation to keep building walls to prevent the poor Latin Americans from entering this country. I have seen the nine-foot high wall in San Diego. It's humiliating for you, as well as for Latin Americans who would like to come here.

José Ramos-Horta: Beyond the question of morality and ethics in weapons sales to developing countries, Western countries usually argue that weapons provisions to some of their client states in developing countries have to do with strategic and security interests—that, for instance, they enhance the security interests of the United States and stability in a given region. And so, regardless of whether they like a regime or not, beyond human rights considerations, they say that we have issues at stake—such as security and stability—that can be enhanced through our military-security relationship with certain countries, certain regimes, as much as we might not like the way they behave. That's the kind of discourse. But what always amazes me is that, even the security and the strategic argument often falls flat, as we saw in at least two cases in 1982. In the Falklands War in Malvinas, it was interesting that the weapons provided by the NATO countries to Argentina—by the British in the past to Argentina, and by the French—ended up colliding with current British weapons in the Atlantic. The famous French Etendard planes, carrying Exocet missiles, sunk British-supplied aircraft and ships that were used by the British in the Falklands war. We saw that weapons in the hands of the dictatorship in the end turned against at least one of the NATO allies in the Falklands war.

Let us consider another most dramatic instance, which threw into question the wisdom of the seemingly most intelligent people in Washington, Paris, and London—I say the most intelligent because, allegedly, you have to be very, very smart to enter the foreign service of these countries since they are the ones who formulate policies and strategic considerations. Look at the case of the Gulf War. The war between Iran and Iraq, we all remember in the eighties; following the collapse of the Shah, Iraq unleashed a war, one of the most vicious wars since World War I, on Iran. At the time Iran was going through an Islamic revolution. You might like it or not, but Iranians have some serious and genuine grievances toward the United States. There is no doubt about that if we look into the history of Iran. Post-Shah Iran was seen as the center of exporting of Islamic fundamentalism; so, Iran was seen as a threat to Western interests. As a result, Saddam Hussein was seen as the ally, the moderating influence in the Gulf region that would stop the spread of Islamic fundamentalism. So all the Western countries supported Saddam Hussein, including transferring technologies for biological weapons. Even when Iranian Kurdish children and women were slaughtered, were killed by gas used for the first time after World War I—we saw thousands of them killed—the West still turned a blind eye. Even when the Iraqi air force by mistake fired on a U.S. warship, killing forty marines, they still found excuses for Saddam Hussein. Then when Iran and Iraq, after ten years of war, exhausted, signed a treaty, and ended the war, Saddam Hussein turned his guns on Kuwait—the same guns that were provided by the West, Russia, and so on. It was only then that Saddam Hussein became evil. I am saying this, not as criticism of those very intelligent people in Washington, heads of state and foreign office, but only as a commoner with a necessarily low IQ—I have to concede that I have a low IQ. I fail to understand those brilliant and strategic considerations that resulted in these fiascoes.

My question to Oscar Arias, as a former head of state, is: when heads of states, policy makers, foreign ministers, look into a given region of the world, look at the map, and then issue a statement about strategic and security considerations, what does it really mean? I am totally at a loss when they said it was in their strategic interests to support Saddam Hussein. Was it really? How did they come to this conclusion?

President Oscar Arias Sánchez: I don't know, José. I don't know. I wonder myself. But again, it is ironic that U.S. weapons have killed American soldiers in Iraq, in Panama, in Somalia—you remember, in Somalia and in many other parts of the world. As long as you keep sending arms to non-democratic countries—I mentioned the figure that 85 percent of the weapons you sell to governments in the developing world go to dictatorships or authoritarian regimes, non-democratic governments—that's the boomerang effect. In the end, it's a moral issue. It was Gandhi who mentioned the seven social sins. Two of them were commerce without morality, and politics without principles. Politics should always go hand-in-hand with morality and with responsibility. It is irresponsible to keep sending arms to dictators. But the U.S. has always considered that there are good and bad dictators. This was acceptable in the Cold War period. Somoza was a good dictator. Trujillo was a good dictator. Ferdinand Marcos was a good dictator. The Shah of Iran was a good dictator. And the bad dictators were Saddam Hussein, Pol Pot, and Fidel Castro for sure. *All* of them are murderers—*all* of them are murderers. The State Department needs indeed to learn that all dictators are bad, and the United States government needs to put morality and principles before profits.

Dr. Rigoberta Menchú Tum: I have doubt when you state that the "educated people" will come out ahead. What is your concept of education and to whom are you referring?

I also want to comment that when we talk about global economies and political globalization, we are talking about material globalization, but we need also to speak about the globalization of problems. For me today, I no longer can see the borders between what once was called the "third world" and what once was called the "first world." I have seen street children in Los Angeles; I have seen poor people in Europe; I can't find at the end of this millennium the difference between the first world, the second world, and the third world.

Also there are other more serious problems: the privatization of state resources benefits people who have already become rich, decreases the capacity of the country's poorest people, and undermines the ability of the government to defend the national sovereignty. The phantom of privatization is a very deep threat against the emerging democracies. As I see it, no democracy has been built in any Latin American country; building democracies is still a goal; it is not something we have reached. We must have a global view of the problems in the present world.

My question is: you said that some people would win and some people would lose, and to me the ones who would lose are the millions and millions of people who have always lost.

President Oscar Arias Sánchez: I mentioned in my remarks this morning that there are 1.3 billion people who earn less than one dollar a day. Those are the poor people of the developing world. The difference, Rigoberta, between the poor people of the developing world and the poor people of the industrialized nations is that the definition of a poor person in the industrialized world is a person earning less than eight thousand to ten thousand dollars per year, instead of one dollar a day in the developing world. The population in this century has quadrupled. It is a fact that by the year 2050 there will be 9 billion people on this planet. Ninety percent of them will be living in the developing world. Sub-Saharan Africa will have a population of 2 billion people. In sub-Saharan African countries the population doubles every twenty years, and sub-Saharan Africa is spending on defense, on the military, five times more now, in 1998, than thirty years ago. Isn't it immoral for the leaders of that continent to prefer to make armed forces a priority over housing, health, education, and basic nutrition for their children? Isn't it immoral for the industrialized nations to keep sending arms to sub-Saharan Africa, to profit by the sale of weapons, instead of helping them? President Clinton just discovered that there is a lot of poverty in sub-Saharan Africa when he visited that continent. There are 700 million people in sub-Saharan Africa, and U.S. aid to that area is $700 million—one dollar per person per year—while you provide Israel, a tiny country of 5 to 6 million people, $3 billion in foreign aid, both economic and military ODA.

How can we deal with populations that double, with countries that double their populations every twenty years? The only way is to cut military spending in order to educate our children. Knowledge is power. Knowledge is wealth. This is obvious for all of you who are well-educated. Every day, every twenty-four hours,

400,000 children are born, 90 percent of them in the developing world. For a high percentage of these children, their destiny is ignorance. Fifty percent of them, in many Latin American countries—Guatemala is one of them—are born from single mothers. What is their destiny? Not to go to school, but to work at the age of twelve, thirteen, fourteen years of age. I want to tell you that even in my own country, which sometimes is represented as some sort of "Switzerland of Central America"—I would prefer to be the "Denmark" of Central America, and not necessarily the "Switzerland" of Central America—but anyway, even in my own country, which does very well in the human development index, 40 percent of our children from thirteen to sixteen years of age do not attend high school. In Guatemala, perhaps it's 80 percent, as well as in Peru, as well as in Nicaragua, as well as in Honduras, as well as in Haiti. In many countries of sub-Saharan Africa, only 5 percent of the children between thirteen and sixteen years of age attend high school. Again, to govern is to choose. If you are uneducated, you will certainly be a loser in a globalized economy, in a globalized world.

Since I have been told by Professor Bond that there is no more time, let me finish by quoting Aristotle—it is always nice to quote the Greeks. He said, "It is not enough to win a war; it is more important to organize the peace. If you do not organize the peace, then you lose the fruits of victory." Let me add one more quote. I keep telling my friends that the U.S. is the only superpower in the world, the only economic superpower, the only military superpower, but the world expects more leadership from you—moral leadership. The world expects the U.S. to become also a moral superpower. The quote is from Albert Einstein: "Only morality in our actions can give beauty and dignity to our lives."

Julian Bond: You have given us a real definition of what leadership is.

Aung San Suu Kyi

Burma

Short Biography

Born in Rangoon, Burma, on June 19, 1945, Aung San Suu Kyi was two years old when her father, General Aung San, was assassinated. While she has no personal memories of him, she is aware of his legacy as the man who helped Burma gain its independence from Great Britain. In fulfillment of an apparent destiny, she is now creating her own legacy as the leading voice for democracy in her troubled country.

Traditionally ruled by Burman monarchs and ethnic chieftains, Aung San Suu Kyi's homeland came under British control in 1885. During the waning years of World War II, Burmese nationalists—led by General Aung San—helped the British defeat Japan in exchange for their country's independence. The general was killed shortly before the British withdrew from Burma in 1948.

A civilian government ruled Burma until 1962, when Burmese General Ne Win staged a coup. His Burma Socialist Programme Party (BSPP) became the official political party in 1974, and Ne Win ruled as the country's prime minister. Before that, he ruled through the Revolutionary Council.

Since then, the Burmese have endured harsh conditions. The country's ethnic minorities have been particularly hard hit. Citizens are arbitrarily executed or imprisoned without judicial due process and have been forced to work as laborers or porters for the army. The army has grown at the expense of education, health care, and social programs, and the forced resettlement of civilians is widespread.

On August 8, 1988, a mass protest by students and workers began in Rangoon and spread into the countryside. The military killed thousands of the unarmed protesters.

Aung San Suu Kyi was in Burma at the time of the uprising to nurse her ailing mother, but for most of her teenage years and young adulthood she had lived abroad. At age fifteen, she accompanied her mother, Daw Khin Kyi, to Delhi, India, where her mother served as the Burmese ambassador to India and Nepal and Aung San Suu Kyi studied politics at Delhi University. From 1964 to 1967, Aung San Suu Kyi lived in England, where she earned a degree in politics, philosophy, and economics from St. Hugh's College, Oxford. After working two foreign posts, she married Dr. Michael Aris, a British Tibetologist. They produced two sons: Alexander, born in London in 1973, and Kim, born in Oxford in 1977.

Aung San Suu Kyi resolved to participate in Burma's "second struggle for national independence." A week after the uprising, she wrote an open letter to the government, calling for multiparty elections. Shortly thereafter, she addressed an estimated half-million people in Rangoon, calling for democracy.

The military retaliated by imposing martial law and creating a new political regime called the State Law and Order Restoration Council (SLORC). The new regime prohibited meetings but not political parties, so Aung San Suu Kyi helped form the National League for Democracy (NLD). As its first general secretary, she held more than a hundred political rallies throughout Burma in 1988. Her message was consistent: resistance through non-violence and reconciliation among the country's feuding ethnic groups. It was also risky; Aung San Suu Kyi narrowly avoided death in April 1989, when a soldier aimed his rifle at her during a rally, only backing down after his superior countermanded the order to fire.

On July 20, 1989, the SLORC placed Aung San Suu Kyi under house arrest initially for three years. Her absence from the NLD did not weaken it. In a free election uncharacteristically held by the SLORC in May 1990, NLD candidates won 82 percent of the national assembly seats. The SLORC refused to recognize the election results. In October, Aung San Suu Kyi was awarded the 1990 Rafto Human Rights Prize.

Under pressure by the United Nations, in December 1990 the SLORC agreed to release Aung San Suu Kyi if she left Burma. She refused to go. On July 11, 1991, she was awarded the Sakharov Prize by the European Parliament for promoting human rights. A month later, the SLORC extended Aung San Suu Kyi's house arrest.

In October, the Norwegian Nobel Committee named Aung San Suu Kyi as its 1991 Peace Prize recipient. "The occasion gives rise to many...conflicting emotions," said Francis Sejersted, committee chairman, in presenting the prize in absentia to her husband and sons. "The Peace Prize Laureate is unable to be here herself. The great work we are acknowledging has yet to be concluded. She is still fighting the good fight."

Using the monetary award that accompanied her prize, Aung San Suu Kyi created a health and education trust fund for the Burmese people in 1992. Her detention was extended a second time in 1994. She was finally released on July 10, 1995, after six years of house arrest.

Gaining her liberty has not meant gaining her freedom. Since 1996, Aung San Suu Kyi has been prevented from speaking or traveling freely. Her country is still ruled by a harsh government. More than one million Burmese have fled their country since the military repression began.

Harn Yawnghwe

Aung San Suu Kyi asked Harn Yawnghwe to participate on her behalf. He is the son of Sao Shwe Thaike, the last hereditary ruler of the Shan principality of Yawnghwe and the first president of the Republic of the Union of Burma.

He was born on April 15, 1948, four months after Burma became an independent nation. After receiving his early education in Burma, he studied in Thailand and then Canada, where he earned a bachelor's degree and an MBA from McGill University.

Through the years, Yawnghwe has faithfully served Burma's pro-democracy movement in a variety of capacities. He was editor of *Burma Alert,* a monthly news digest; advisor to Dr. Sein Win, prime minister of the National Coalition Government of the Union of Burma; and managing director of the Democratic Voice of Burma, which makes daily news broadcasts to Burma in Burmese and seven ethnic languages.

In February 1997, he became director of the Euro-Burma Office in Brussels, Belgium. This joint project between the European Union and the German Friedrich Ebert Foundation was created to help the Burmese democracy movement prepare for a transition to a democratic government.

Yawnghwe, who is now a Canadian citizen, makes his home in Brussels with his wife and two children.

HARN YAWNGHWE, *participating for* AUNG SAN SUU KYI
"The U.N. Declaration of Human Rights and
Its Impact on Asian Values and Democratic Principles"

Professor Bond, distinguished guests, ladies and gentlemen, it is a signal honor for me to be asked by Daw Aung San Suu Kyi to participate in this conference on her behalf. It is really a great honor to be addressing such an eminent panel and such a learned audience. I hope I can do it justice.

It has been a great learning experience for me; I have really been enriched by the time here. I am only sorry that Daw Aung San Suu Kyi is not present. She would have really enjoyed the company and fellowship of her fellow Nobel Laureates, and she would have enjoyed the intellectual challenge.

The fact that she is not here highlights the situation in Burma. I did not properly address the question that was asked yesterday why she is not present. I took it for granted that people knew the situation. The reality is that although she is supposed to be free, she is not. How can you say she is free when she cannot meet with her husband and her children? They cannot visit her. They are not given visas by the military junta. She cannot get on the telephone to talk to them because not only is the telephone line tapped when it is working, most of the time it is cut. And even when it is not cut, when she talks to people, if the military thinks that the subject is not appropriate, they will cut the line.

Apart from that, she cannot, as a leader of her party, move about freely to talk to members of her party, or even with executives of her party. And not everybody can just walk in to visit her—there are troops around, the roads are blocked, there are security agents all over the place. Is that freedom? Would you consider it freedom if you could not move around, see your friends? Still, the military is saying that she was released from house arrest in 1995.

It is ironic that while I am here to talk about a key U.N. document, the Universal Declaration of Human Rights, the U.N.—according to the British Broadcasting Corporation—is considering a "carrot" plan to give aid to the military. Of course, they say, you have to offer incentives to make them negotiate. But as we heard yesterday from His Grace, Archbishop Desmond Tutu, who has lived through a struggle for freedom, "You need to keep the sanctions. Without the sanctions, we could not have achieved what we have achieved." I just bring this to you to underline the concern we have and the real need not to relax. Dr. Sein Win, who is Daw Aung San Suu Kyi's political representative, is the Prime Minister of the government-in-exile. He is currently at the U.N. trying to persuade the U.N. that maybe they should go slow—this is not the right time for monetary incentives to the military junta which, according to the BBC, would be large World Bank loans. I am bringing this to your attention before my talk so that you are aware, you are briefed of the need to caution the United Nations that they are moving too fast. Even in South Africa, the sanctions were not lifted until way after the changes were in place. In Burma, the military isn't even talking with Aung San Suu Kyi yet; so how can we even be thinking of renewing aid? I am sorry for going off the topic, but I felt strongly that you need to know about this.

If Daw Aung San Suu Kyi were here, she would be very happy, and I'm sure she would want me to express her gratitude and her appreciation, especially to Professor Hopkins and to the University of Virginia, as well as to Michele Bohana, for this great opportunity. It is hard to express the comfort we get from such support and such solidarity. I would also like to use the occasion to personally thank Betty Williams, Archbishop Desmond Tutu, President Oscar Arias, His Holiness the Dalai Lama, and Rigoberta Menchú Tum, because in 1993—it was unprecedented—they got together with other Nobel Peace Laureates and went to Thailand on behalf of their sister laureate. Unfortunately, they were not allowed to travel to Burma, but they showed their concern for their fellow laureate by visiting the Thai-Burma border. I would also like to further thank Bishop Tutu, President Oscar Arias, and José Ramos-Horta for their recent declaration with other Nobel Laureates, not just the Peace Laureates, on behalf of Burma. The support is incredible, and I am constantly amazed. Thank you.

Now, I will go on to the topic I was asked to speak about. As you know, debates about the Universal Declaration of Human Rights and Asian values have almost always been portrayed as an East-West values conflict. Prime Minister Dr. Mahathir Mohamad of Malaysia has said that the Declaration "is formulated by the superpowers which did not understand the needs of the poor countries." As such, he is implying that the Universal Declaration is not applicable to Asia and the poor countries. It should be mentioned that in fact this is not true. The initiative for the Universal Declaration of Human Rights did not start with governments; American civic organizations and non-governmental organizations lobbied for human rights to be recognized within the U.N., so that it did not fall into the same trap as the League of Nations. Because of that, human rights became a major component of the U.N. Charter, and from that, it led to the formation of the U.N. Commission on Human Rights. The special committee formed to draft the Universal Declaration had eight members. Apart from the Soviet Union, France, the United Kingdom, and the United States, it included Australia, China, Chile, and Lebanon. Of course, China, at that time, was not the People's Republic, but the composition shows that the Declaration did reflect Asian values as well.

When the Declaration was adopted in 1948, the U.N. had fifty-six member countries; forty-eight countries voted for it, and eight countries abstained. Among the eight countries that abstained, six were from the Soviet Bloc, and the other two were Saudi Arabia and South Africa. So, the world has changed. The countries that endorsed the Declaration were Burma, China, Cuba, India, Iran, Iraq, the Philippines, and Thailand. In actuality, the smaller countries in the third world were very enthusiastic about the Declaration because this was the first international agreement recognizing the equality and dignity of all peoples, regardless of the size of their country, regardless of their geographic or ethnic origin. And U Thant, a Burmese who was the Secretary-General of the United Nations in the sixties, said that the Universal Declaration is the Magna Carta of humankind. Yet, today, we have the generals in Burma saying that the U.N. Declaration doesn't fit our values, that it's being imposed on us by Westerners.

Another argument used by the people who push Asian values is that they were not members when the Declaration was adopted, so they shouldn't be forced to accept the Universal Declaration of Human Rights. That argument is not valid, because if you join an organization, you should know what the organization stands for, and since the Universal Declaration is a key document, it is senseless to say that you were not a member when it was adopted.

As for Asian values, I would like to start by saying, "What values are we talking about?" If you say "Asian values," which ones? As far as I know, the term "Asian values" was not invented by an Asian; it was invented by a Western economist who could not understand what was happening in the economies of Asia, so he said, "There is something abnormal here, it doesn't fit the theory, so it must be 'Asian values.'"

Since then, the term has been used by many people to mean many different things. Former Prime Minister Lee Kuan Yew of Singapore—the former prime minister and current senior minister, whatever that means—popularized the idea of "Asian values." He was, at the time, talking specifically about East Asia, meaning the countries of Japan, China, Taiwan, Singapore, and Hong Kong; he was saying that these countries have done well economically because of Asian values, and that means, according to him, that they place group interests over individual interests. His argument gained credibility when in 1993 the World Conference on Human Rights in Vienna took it as a valid argument and discussed it officially. Also, the Bangkok Declaration, which was a preparation for that conference, stated that "Human rights must be considered in the context of national and regional peculiarities and various historical, cultural and religious backgrounds." That's what these governments say—we do not agree. The peoples of Asia had an alternative conference, at which they rejected this notion.

But, be that as it may, is there really a distinct set of Asian values that are different from Western values, if there is such a thing? Because when you talk about the West, we know that the United States is very different from Europe, and, in Europe itself, you have very different cultures and different values—from the Nordic countries, to the Mediterranean, to the Slavic countries. Just take the United States, you have very different values among different groups. So, what Western values are we talking about? And what Asian values are we talking about? As I said before, Lee Kuan Yew was only talking about the so-called "East Asian countries." What about "South Asian values"—India, Pakistan, Sri Lanka, Bangladesh? What about the Malay Polynesian values in Indonesia, Malaysia, Papua New Guinea—all these countries?

Even in Burma, where we have many ethnic groups, we have very different values. If you are living on the plains and are a rice farmer, or if you are living in the hills and you are a hunter, you have very different values. So, what values are we talking about? Some of the people who argue that "East-West" values are different also say, "The problem really is Western Christian values being imposed on Asians." But again, you have to remember that the Asian values debate that Lee Kuan Yew used was based only on Confucianism, which is very different again, and it does not touch on the values that the rest of Asia have, which are Buddhist, Muslim, Hindu, Christian, and also animist. And to top it all off, if you really look at Christian values, basic Christian values without all the cultural overtones, these are not Western values, they are from the Middle East. They have the same root as Islam and Judaism. On top of that, there are more Christians today in Asia and Africa than in the so-called Western world. And there are many Hindus, many Buddhists, and many Muslims in the Western world. So, what are we really talking about?

Others have said it's a question of traditions versus liberal democracy, or it is a question of society versus individual rights, or that it is a question of spiritual values versus material values. But, as with religion, Asian traditions are diverse. Societal values, spiritual values, as I mentioned, are also very different across Asia. It's not a monolithic block. Also, we cannot always claim that traditions are good. Slavery, the status of women, the degradation of women in some cultures, these are traditions. Does that mean that we should tolerate these traditions? On the other hand, preserving our culture, preserving our traditions, does not mean that human rights have to be denied. It is not an either/or question, because, even in traditional societies in Asia, there are limits. We do not tolerate abuse of power. Even a king, in the olden days, if he abused his power, was not tolerated for very long. Even the Confucian belief that Lee Kuan Yew quoted does not advocate blind allegiance to the state. President Kim Dae-Jung of South Korea has been an advocate on our side who has also shown that Confucianism is not what Lee Kuan Yew claims it to be.

Also, we have great traditions. For example: in India, the Emperor Ashoka, who ruled before Christ, before the third century B.C.E., was a Hindu who became a Buddhist and is well known for his enlightened politics. The principles of good governance and tolerance of diversity in societal and religious behavior were known since thousands of years ago. The same with Emperor Akbar. He was a Moghul emperor, a Muslim. He too was known for his kingship, for his good governance. The same can be said of Burma. We have something called "The Ten Duties of Kings" which is widely accepted as the yardstick for good government. They are: liberality, morality, self-sacrifice, integrity, kindness, austerity, non-anger, non-violence, forbearance, and, most important of all, non-opposition to the will of the people. You can read about this in Daw Aung San Suu Kyi's book *Freedom from Fear.* She has expanded on this. So, Burmese Buddhist traditions are compatible with the Universal Declaration of Human Rights.

Therefore, it is quite meaningless to be talking about an East/West values conflict, and Asian values. This is especially true in the case of Burma. The people of Burma want democracy. This was made abundantly clear in the 1990 elections, which, by the way, were organized by the military. Daw Aung San Suu Kyi's National League for Democracy won 82 percent of the seats in Parliament. What government today can boast such a majority? The military-backed party won 2 percent of the seats and that was why they did not honor the election results.

You can see that the Burmese people want democracy, but we have heard that the democracy movement is influenced by Western values. If you really look at it, although we had the election in 1990, Burma has been a country isolated for the last thirty-five years. The military took over in 1962, and they blocked off contact with the rest of the world. So, how can the people of Burma, who have had no contact with the Western world for over thirty years, be influenced by Western values? The media—all media in Burma—are controlled by the military. We have no cable television; we have no satellite TV—it is illegal to have a satellite dish. We have no access to the Internet. In fact, a Burmese citizen who was the Consul General of Denmark was arrested for having a fax machine. They arrested him, denied him treatment—he was an old man with a heart condition—they denied him medical care; he died in prison. This is a person who was a diplomat, accredited to a foreign government, not only Denmark but also several European governments.

So, how were the Burmese people influenced by Western values? They have no access to the West; yet, they want democracy. In the case of Burma, the theory pushed on us by some clever people is: "To have a democracy you first need to have economic development, because you can't have a democracy without a middle class; you need a large middle class." The people of Burma are peasants; I would say about 85 percent of the country lives off agriculture. We have very few people in the cities and a very small middle class. Yet, when the people voted, they knew what they wanted. Why is this? It is because, through their own experience of three decades of military rule they have seen that a small elite should not be left to make all the decisions and be unaccountable for their actions. What is good for the generals has not been good for Burma and the people. We used to be one of the richest countries in Southeast Asia. We are richer in resources than Thailand, but today we are one of the ten poorest nations in the world. People in Burma want democracy because they want to limit the power of their rulers. They want to be able to have rulers who are accountable, who are responsible, and who will be responsive to the needs of the people. That has nothing to do with being middle class, or being influenced by Western values. At this point, I would like to remind all of us that democracy is not a Western monopoly. The largest and one of the longest functioning democracies in the world today is India. It is an Asian nation that has traditions going back many thousands of years, and yet it is a democracy. It's not perfect, but it functions.

I would like to say that this is ample evidence that democracy and human rights are not at odds with Asian values and are not at odds with Asian cultures and traditions. Of course, we are not advocating an American-style democracy; even in the "West," you have very different kinds of democracies, democratic systems, electoral systems—all kinds of rules and laws that are different. As Daw Aung San Suu Kyi said, "What I want to see is the peaceful transition to a political system which is in accordance with the will of the majority." That is what we want, and democracy is the nearest thing to it.

Then, the question is, why has this position of separate "Asian values" gained such credibility? It was Lee Kuan Yew who proposed it first, and the conference discussed it, but what is really behind this argument? In this context, I would like to quote the Secretary-General of the United Nations, Mr. Kofi Annan. He is not a Westerner; he was speaking about the freedom of speech:

There are those who still question the value of freedom of speech, those who still consider freedom of speech an imposition from abroad and not the indigenous expression of every people's demand for freedom. What has always struck me about this argument is that it is never made by the people, but by the governments. Never by the powerless, but by the powerful. Never by the voiceless, but by those whose voices are all that can be heard.

I believe the Secretary-General has captured the intentions behind what the Asian leaders are arguing when they say that human rights are Western values. What they have glossed over is the fact that the Universal Declaration really is just an attempt to ensure that all people—regardless of their background, their sex, or other differences—are treated equally, that everybody is treated with dignity, and to ensure that they are protected by the rule of law, that they can live free from fear, and be able to speak freely. It is hard for me to comprehend why it is so difficult for some of these rulers to accept that people should be treated equally, regardless of who or what they are. If we accept that basic human rights are universal, we can solve many problems—not only in Burma but especially in Burma because we have many ethnic groups who are fighting the military dictatorship and they are not fighting for anything more than to be treated as human beings.

To encourage you, I would like to give you a practical example of how applying the Universal Declaration can work. You may not be aware of it, but I am not from the same ethnic group as Daw Aung San Suu Kyi. She is a Burman, I am a Shan. Apart from that, my father and her father were on opposite sides of the table when they were negotiating to form modern Burma. They were able to agree, in 1947—before the Universal Declaration—that the basis for all the different ethnic groups joining Burma to gain independence from Britain would be equality. All the races of Burma would be equal, and they would participate voluntarily in the Union of Burma. That is right in line with the Universal

Declaration. Unfortunately, General Aung San, Daw Aung San Suu Kyi's father, was assassinated before we got independence, and, in a sense, the ethnic people were betrayed because the agreement with General Aung San was not fully implemented. In the aftermath of independence, my father did try to bring about the agreement, but the military said that amending the constitution peacefully would break up the country; so, instead, they launched a coup. I lost one of my brothers; ours was the only house that the military surrounded and opened fire on—one of my brothers was killed. My father was arrested, taken to prison, and he died eight months later, in solitary confinement. My mother was nearly arrested, but luckily she was away and she escaped—we all escaped, finally. I have been a refugee when the only thing I possessed were the clothes on my back. But, I have recovered, and I am working with a Burman. You could say the agreement with my father was not honored, and maybe I could accuse Aung San Suu Kyi and the Burmese leadership of betrayal, but that is not the way it works. I know that she stands for the universality of human rights. She stands for democracy, for the people to decide. And I am proud to have been asked by her to represent her today. I think it is a very hopeful sign. We will overcome.

Thank you.

Discussion Among the Participants

Julian Bond: Recently, we have seen some expressions of public dissatisfaction with regimes in Indonesia and Malaysia, but not so in Burma. We understand that there is rigid control.

Harn Yawnghwe: There has been dissatisfaction and some protest, but it has been small, and it has not caught the attention of the media. One of the reasons, for example, that you haven't seen more activity is that Burmese students at the University of Rangoon demonstrated against the regime in December of 1996, and in order to control demonstrations, the regime closed down universities. They have been closed since December 1996. Can you imagine that? One university demonstrated, and the whole country is shut down. There are no universities operating in Burma today. At the time of the student demonstrations, they also closed down the high schools, because high school students were supporting the university students. This is the extent of control.

The labor movement? It doesn't exist in Burma. It is illegal to have a union. It is illegal for more than four people to gather. Military intelligence is everywhere. Many of the leaders of the priesthood, the Buddhist Sangha, are also in prison. As I said, the media is controlled. Even Daw Aung San Suu Kyi, whose party is recognized as having won the election, cannot move around—she cannot talk to ordinary people. That's why it has been very difficult. There have been protests now and again, and students have tried to protest, but they are very quickly put down.

Dr. Rigoberta Menchú Tum: I would like to know more about the refugees from Burma in Thailand. Some years ago, I had the opportunity of being with them, and I was very struck by the condition of their life, by the lack of liberty that they have in Thailand. Many of us want to read all about this, but there is very, very little information about this. And I would also like to know more about political refugees.

Harn Yawnghwe: Unfortunately, I have to say that, since your visit, the situation for the refugees on the Thai border has gotten worse. There have been attacks from across the Burmese border, and refugee camps have been burned. People have been kidnapped from refugee camps. The Thai government has tried to make conditions safer by consolidating camps, but this has increased restrictions on the refugees. This year, the Thai government invited the United Nations High Commission for Refugees to be present on the border. In one way, it could help if the U.N. is present on the border, but we are also concerned, because we know that among the Thai military, who are charged with looking after the security of the camps, there are also those who feel that if the refugees were not in Thailand, there would not be any problems. Their idea to secure Thailand's border is to push the refugees back into Burma.

You might think, "If the UNHCR is there, maybe that's a good thing," but we are not so sure, because in the early 1990s, we had 300,000 refugees from the Arakan State, Muslim Rohingas, who fled to Bangladesh, after which they were repatriated to Burma by the UNHCR. They said it was a voluntary repatriation, but we have heard that the refugees were not told that they had any choice. The other problem with repatriation is that in theory, when you repatriate a refugee, he or she should be able to reintegrate back into the community and be able to live in freedom. Nobody in Burma lives in freedom. They are subject to forced labor, brutality from the military—women are raped, people are killed on the spot for small offenses. And further, people are not reintegrated into society—they live in camps on the Burmese side of the border. So, what is the sense of repatriation? We would like to see the UNHCR present, but they need to protect the refugees, they need to monitor the situation, not oblige governments or armies.

José Ramos-Horta: From your words, and from what we all have read and known about Burma, my conclusion is that the situation in Burma is even worse than in the worst years of the Suharto regime in Indonesia. As much as we, from East Timor, have been on the receiving end of one of the worst wars of aggression in modern history, even during the Suharto regime—we have had ongoing Internet activity in East Timor, except on a few occasions when computers and fax machines were seized. I, personally, never called for comprehensive sanctions against Indonesia as such—except for the boycott of certain American-made products because of the exploitation of cheap labor in Indonesia—since I believe that economic engagement, sometimes, with some countries, in certain circumstances, can be helpful. This, to some extent, was the case with Indonesia, with the exception of the behavior of Nike, for instance, which exploited poverty and justified it by saying, "Well, if we are not there, they won't have jobs, so let's exploit them." That's one of the elements I disagree with.

Because most of Oscar's and my own contributions here seem to be overcritical, or very critical, of U.S. policies, I think sometimes it is fair to say that, though modestly, it is the United States that has taken the lead. We, along with the European Union—the Norwegians in particular—are putting pressure on the Burmese. As I was tuning in to CNN this morning, I was really touched and impressed to hear that American cargo planes are getting ready to go to Honduras to deliver humanitarian assistance to Central America. That's one of the good things this country does. It occurred to me: what better thing could President Clinton do now, if he were to fly to Central America and visit those countries and draw even more attention to the needs in those countries. Or Hillary Clinton could do that.

Back to Burma: I am always confused why the so-called Helms-Burton Act—not that I agree with the Helms-Burton Act on Cuba—couldn't be used on Burma? The situation in Burma is far worse than in Cuba. I agree that human rights violations are human rights violations, and in this sense we cannot say one is better and one is worse, but if sanctions are justified with respect to Cuba, why are they not taking steps forward to apply the principle of the Helms-Burton Act to Burma? What I mean to say is that there are certain countries in the region that are circumventing the limited sanctions on Burma, thereby allowing the Burmese junta to continue surviving. One is China, the major military backer and economic backer of Burma. The other ones were Singapore—now with the economic collapse in the region, maybe they are not so enthusiastic about Burma—and the other one was Indonesia. In this respect the domino collapse was fortunate. My question to Harn, and maybe to Julian Bond and others who are more familiar with U.S. policies toward Burma, is: why isn't the U.S. taking steps toward warning the countries in the region—China, Singapore—to cease their support of the Burmese junta? What is to prevent the U.S. from taking an additional step? I am sure Secretary of State Madeleine Albright must be one of the persons who must understand very well and admire their fellow woman leader, Daw Aung San Suu Kyi, and that Dr. Albright would use her power to really support the struggle in Burma.

Harn Yawnghwe: Thank you. I would like to say that, as José said, in the case of Burma, we have no complaints about U.S. government policy. They have been very, very supportive. When the U.S. ambassador who was in Burma finished his term after 1988, the U.S. did not replace him; they downgraded relations. There is no foreign aid to the regime; there is an arms embargo; and since early 1997 President Clinton has enacted legislation which prevents American firms from making new investments in Burma. So, we do have sanctions from the U.S. In addition to the sanctions, we have visa bans. High-level military junta officials and their families cannot visit the U.S. The U.S. lead has caused other nations, including the European Union, to adopt similar measures. The only thing we don't have in Europe is the invest-ment ban. We almost got it; the European Union was willing to enact a similar ban, but France vetoed it because they have a major investment in Burma with Unocal in southern Burma building a gas pipeline, and that gas pipeline actually has caused untold mis-eries to the people living in that area. So, we do have some things, but, I believe, one of the reasons something like Helms-Burton is not pushed, is that you now have something called the World Trade Organization, and you are not supposed to hinder world trade. Nevertheless, the state of Massachusetts and several cities in the states have adopted selected purchasing, meaning that they will not give city or state contracts to companies doing business in

Burma. Many, many companies have pulled out because of this legislation, and Massachusetts, very bravely, was the first state to adopt it. Unfortunately, because of the World Trade Organization, the European Union and Japan are bringing the state of Massachusetts to task for going against the World Trade Organization. At the same time, U.S. corporations, under the banner of USA-Engage, fearing that the example of Burma and the state of Massachusetts will lead to other sanctions—state and city sanctions against Indonesia and China—have banded together to sue the state of Massachusetts. It is currently before the court.

Julian Bond: We are pleased to hear that there is a movement for democracy that has no complaints against the United States!

Questions from the Audience

Jeffrey Hopkins: First, I would like to thank President Arias for his clear presentation of the stark facts and figures of arms proliferation; we all need to hear this. And I want to thank Harn Yawnghwe for his provocatively profound questioning of popular but foolish boundaries. The first question is addressed to President Arias. A big part of the pressure to sell arms comes from arms dealers, big companies with big lobbying budgets, pushing government, defense, and foreign aid budgets. How can we intervene against this lobby?

President Oscar Arias Sánchez: As I mentioned, it is very unfortunate that there has not been the political will to approve the International Code of Conduct on Arms Transfers. This is the only way to restrict the sale of arms to dictatorships, to violators of human rights, to governments which are involved in armed aggression against other nations, to governments which sponsor terrorism, to governments which do not comply with the U.N. Register of Conventional Arms, etc. These are well known. As I said, it is a matter of principles or profits. It's a matter of values. It's a matter of morality. These people are very powerful; they make huge contributions, huge donations, to congresspersons; these are well known. Very few Americans, as I mentioned, are aware that the American taxpayer is subsidizing arms exports, that the arms you manufacture need to be exported, because the Pentagon doesn't need them. I usually make a parallel between the sale of arms and the sale of drugs. The sale of drugs is illegal, the sale of arms is legal. In Washington, they look at the supply side in the case of drugs for the countries which are producing drugs and exporting them to wealthy nations. In the case of arms, they look at the demand side, and they tell me, "If there is a country willing to buy arms from us, we will sell them, because otherwise, any other country will sell them." However, the fact that the sale of drugs is illegal and the sale of arms is legal doesn't make the sale of arms morally right. Both kill people. Both kill innocent young children. What would a Burmese say, or a Colombian, or a Bolivian, if you tell him, "Don't send drugs to America"? I believe the Burmese would tell you, "If I don't sell drugs to you, Bolivia will, Peru will." That's the answer I get from the United States: "If I don't sell arms to you, France will, Russia will, China will."

Jeffrey Hopkins: This question is for Harn Yawnghwe. Is Aung San Suu Kyi able to make use of the funds contributed to the Health and Education Trust Fund that she set up for the Burmese people in 1992?

Harn Yawnghwe: Yes. She used the money from the Nobel Peace Prize to form the foundation, and it is now being used for scholarships so that they can get an education and be prepared for the future.

Jeffrey Hopkins: This is a question for José Ramos-Horta. Who have been the most influential people in your life?

José Ramos-Horta: Well, it's a very difficult question. I was always very, very fond of, and a great admirer of the Kennedys. As a teenager, I admired John Kennedy, Robert Kennedy, and Ted Kennedy, and now I am also a good friend of Patrick Kennedy. It is remarkable, interesting how—far away in Timor, we had no television, only some very bad short-wave radio—we heard a lot about John Kennedy and Robert Kennedy. They influenced me a lot. Then came, obviously later on, Martin Luther King. And then, among the living ones: this gentleman sitting opposite—His Holiness the Dalai Lama. When first I heard about the Dalai Lama, it was simple curiosity. The name was exotic, the country was exotic; everybody spoke so much about the Dalai Lama that I went to listen to His Holiness. I was among the first to line up, because I wanted to see him up close. After a half-hour, I left. I was bored! Because he kept talking about peace and peace and I wanted to hear more about his trip from Tibet to exile. But then when I left the meeting, I kept thinking about how this man, to whom the Chinese authorities have done so much harm—to him and to his people—was so compassionate. And then I started thinking more seriously about his words, and began reading more: [John Avedon's] *In Exile from the Land of Snows.* It made me very embarrassed when—at that time—I would hate the Indonesians and would love to see someone bombing Jakarta; then I would become embarrassed. I learned tremendously from His Holiness.

But the list of people I admire is enormous. Tremendous inspirations, lessons from Oscar Arias, Desmond Tutu and so many others—Daw Aung San Suu Kyi. So I could not say one particular person, because, fortunately, there are so many. But the very first that affected me, probably, unlike most people, were the Kennedys.

Jeffrey Hopkins: The final question is for Dr. Menchú Tum. One commentator recently said that the devastation wrought by Hurricane Mitch last week would set Central American development back twenty years. Would you agree, and how should the U.S. respond?

Dr. Rigoberta Menchú Tum: Yes, Unfortunately, in the case of both Honduras and Guatemala, 80 percent of the national territory is incommunicado; we have no contact with those areas, we really don't know what has happened and how serious the situation there is. There have been a lot of mudslides, a lot of rivers have overflowed their banks and have taken entire towns and villages with them. There are various towns and communities throughout Central America with which our foundation, La Fundación Rigoberta Menchú Tum, works, but unfortunately we have not been able to establish contact with our companions in those communities. In Guatemala, we have four *compañeros* of the Foundation itself, with whom we have not been able to establish contact, either with them, or with their families. They may be safe somewhere, but we do not know what their present situation is.

What is patently clear is that our people were not prepared to receive this devastation, because the people are poor, they are so very, very poor. So, I really can't say what the repercussions are going to be until we are able to find out more clearly and more systematically what has actually happened. There have been many, many people who have been killed, and it is very sad that the mayor of Tegucigalpa, the capital city of Honduras, has also died. We have been making calls in order to encourage people to help, and to support. Any help that people can give will be crucially important in our endeavor to reconstruct these countries.

I would like to say that we all, finally, have the obligation to help in this sense because we have all contributed to the destruction of nature. One of the repercussions of this destruction of Mother Earth is this unbalancing. As you know, we are in Guatemala, the Foundation is there, and we are working with many different organizations to help those who are suffering.

President Oscar Arias Sánchez: The best way you can help Central America is by opening up the U.S. market for our goods, industrialized goods, and agricultural goods. Ironically, the U.S. Congress is in favor of the expansion of NATO, so that U.S. weapons can be sold to the Czech Republic, to Hungary, and to Poland; but it is not in favor of the expansion of NAFTA, even though everybody in this country talks about free trade and how important free trade is for developing nations. In other words, what is preached is not practiced.

Also, I just want to mention because the audience might not know, even though foreign aid is a very unpopular concept in this country, you are responsible for the revival of Europe with the Marshall Plan. The Marshall Plan implied, I believe, at that time, 3 or 4 percent of GDP to the destroyed nations of Europe. Now, fifty years later, among the industrialized nations, you are channeling to the developing countries much less than any other industrialized nation. As a matter of fact, it is only one-tenth of what the Dutch, the Norwegians, the Swedes, the Danish, spend on official development assistance to poor nations. Just one-tenth. Nevertheless, the American public believe it is a huge percentage of your gross national product and of the federal budget; this is not true. Even in absolute terms, France, Germany, and Japan allocate more funds to foreign aid to the developing world than the U.S. Finally, it is ironic and sad that only ten years ago, when the bloody conflict occurred in Central America, you were channeling huge amounts of foreign aid to those countries during the years of the Cold War, but now that the Central American countries have had the courage and vision to silence the guns at the negotiating table—now that we have been able to bring peace to thirty million Central Americans who did not deserve to live in conflict—instead of being rewarded for the peace we have achieved, we have been punished by the U.S. cutting all foreign aid to the five Central American countries. This, indeed, cannot be understood, I believe, by anybody.

Bobby Muller

Co-founder of the International Campaign to Ban Landmines

The International Campaign to Ban Landmines, 1997 Nobel Peace Co-Laureate

Landmines don't discriminate. They kill or maim civilians just as easily as they do soldiers. They cost as little as three dollars apiece to manufacture, yet up to one thousand dollars apiece to remove. Consequently, an estimated 110 million landmines remain embedded in the soil of sixty-eight countries, with another 2 million buried each year. They claim twenty-six thousand victims annually—many curious children, such as the Egyptian girl who was killed early in 1998 by a landmine that had been buried in the desert by Rommel's Afrika Korps in 1942.

In 1991 Bobby Muller, president of the Vietnam Veterans of American Foundation (VVAF), vowed to do something about the landmine problem. He began discussions with medico international, a German-based humanitarian group, about founding an international campaign to ban landmines that would rely on the lobbying efforts of non-governmental organizations, or NGOs, like theirs. He recruited activist Jody Williams to coordinate the effort.

The International Campaign to Ban Landmines (ICBL) was formally launched in October 1992 with six NGOs. As word of the campaign spread, the numbers and effectiveness of the NGOs grew exponentially. In March 1995, Belgium became the first nation to adopt a landmine ban.

Less than six years after the ICBL started, Canada invited world leaders to convene in Ottawa in December 1997 to sign a comprehensive treaty banning the use, production, transfer, and stockpiling of landmines. More than one hundred countries agreed to attend. Several military powers, including the United States, remained uncommitted; they cited concerns that a total landmine ban would imperil their soldiers, many of whom were stationed in known combat zones.

The Norwegian Nobel Committee was a keen observer of this process. In October 1997 it awarded the Nobel Peace Prize jointly to the International Campaign to Ban Landmines and its coordinator, Jody Williams, stating that they had "started a process which in the space of a few years changed a ban on antipersonnel mines from a vision to a feasible reality."

The committee's decision was also intended to pressure the United States and other recalcitrant countries to endorse the proposed treaty. "Many nations, among them the largest, have been reluctant, at least so far, to commit themselves to not using this weapon...," said Francis Sejersted, chairman of the Norwegian Nobel Committee, when giving the prize to the ICBL and Williams. "Let us therefore... express the hope that the process will win still greater support, so that the work can be intensified and a world without antipersonnel mines can become a reality in the foreseeable future."

Even without the endorsement of the United States, China, most Middle Eastern nations, and Russia (which said it would support the ban the day after the 1997 Nobel Peace Prize was announced), Muller's vision for a landmine-free world was affirmed. On December 4, 1997, 121 countries—including nearly every state in Latin America, Africa, and the European Union—became signatories to the Ottawa Treaty. Three of those countries, Canada, Mauritius, and Ireland, ratified the treaty upon signature. The others are now in the process of doing so through their legislatures. Six months after the fortieth country ratified, the landmine ban became international law.

Since Ottawa, the ICBL has successfully lobbied six other countries to sign the treaty. The United States has now committed to signing the treaty by 2006 and has advanced a "2010 Initiative" that calls for the international community to provide ten billion dollars in de-mining funding over a period of ten years. The goal of this initiative is to begin the long process of identifying, removing, and destroying the millions of landmines that remain in the ground in developing countries.

In May 1998, Muller and the VVAF launched the Campaign for a Landmine Free World, which will help fulfill the goals of the Ottawa Treaty by surveying landmine areas, assisting victims, and educating the public about the menace of landmines. Mine removal will have a positive impact on developing countries like Angola, Cambodia,
and Afghanistan, all of which could increase their agricultural production by at least one-third if the cropland was cleared of antipersonnel mines.

Short Biography of Bobby Muller

Robert O. (Bobby) Muller was born in 1945. After graduating from Hofstra University with a degree in business administration, he enlisted in the U.S. Marine Corps and served as an infantry officer in Vietnam in 1968 and 1969. A combat injury rendered him paraplegic.

He returned to the United States and became an active opponent of the Vietnam War, as well as a crusader for veterans' rights. In 1974 he earned a second degree from Hofstra, this one in law.

In 1978, he founded the Vietnam Veterans of America (VVA). As president of VVA, he led a veterans delegation to Vietnam in 1981—the first such delegation to visit the country since the end of the war—and spearheaded efforts to establish court review of veterans' benefits and to preserve and expand veterans' counseling services.

In 1980, he helped establish the Vietnam Veterans of America Foundation (VVAF), an international humanitarian organization providing aid to the victims of war, and, in 1987, became its president. Through the VVAF, he has established clinics to manufacture and distribute wheelchairs and artificial limbs to those who have lost limbs as the result of landmines. He led the effort to create the International Campaign to Ban Landmines and founded the U.S. Campaign to Ban Landmines. Most recently, he launched the Campaign for a Landmine Free World, which will aid in fulfilling the goals of the international landmine ban treaty signed in December 1997.

Muller has lectured at more than one hundred universities and colleges on the lessons learned from the Vietnam experience and the relevance of those lessons for the U.S. role in the international community.

BOBBY MULLER
"The Vietnam Veterans of America Foundation and the International Campaign to Ban Landmines"

It's been a real privilege for me to be here and to meet the people who are on stage, but I want to tell you something: quite a few of these folks are very regular people. Just like you. Perhaps in no case would that apply more than to me. I wouldn't have been in the audience here, when I was in college. I would have been doing some-thing with an athletic event or focused in maybe on my studies. I was the most average student that you could ever imagine. Had you suggested that I would one day be appearing on a platform with people such as this, I would have said, "You're crazy."

What happened? I become an advocate as a result of my life's experiences. If there's anything I'm going to urge students in par-ticular to do, it's to get a little less homogenized, and get out there in the world, and expose yourself to different situations, because I believe relatively few among us can intellectually arrive at a cer-tain place of enlightenment. To get it a little bit, most of us need to go out there and get the hard knocks in life, learn the lessons the hard way.

I got it because when I was a senior in college, the war in Viet-nam was going on full-tilt boogie. It was inevitable that I was going to go into the service, and one day, I was going into the student union my senior year. I was 5' 8", 130 pounds; I was the ultimate runt, and there was the Marine Corps recruiter—he stood around 6' 2", 220 pounds, dress blue uniform, crimson stripe—ultimate stud—and I said, "Yeah, that's me." Honestly—I hate to admit it—that machismo thing that kids have, on the basis of the impression of that uniform, I joined the Marines.

As I said yesterday, you should see a movie, *Full Metal Jacket,* that Kubrick put out. The first half of the movie is about Marine Corps boot camp; it shows you how young guys can be trans-formed as a result of a process—that we are very vulnerable, sus-ceptible to being altered and manipulated. The long and the short of it is, by the time I finished my Marine Corps training—I gradu-ated Honor Man in my class—I demanded Vietnam, I demanded infantry, and my only fear was that the war was going to end before I got a chance to get over there and do the right thing.

A long story made very short: there were more U.S. Marine casualties in Vietnam than there were U.S. Marine casualties in the entire Second World War. When I was in training, they said 85 percent of us, as junior officers, were going to be casualties. I went out into the field with seven other lieutenants, all of whom were medevacked before me. I lasted eight months before I took a bullet through the chest. That war was a rock 'em, sock 'em war. When I got hit, I had the good fortune of having called in medevac helicopters for other guys that had become casualties, so I got, literally, an instant medical evacuation. With my luck, the hospital ship Repose was right off the coast from where I was that afternoon, and they wrote that, despite the instant medevac, and the extraordinary care, had I arrived one minute later, I would have died. Both lungs had collapsed, along with a severed spinal cord. I was conscious long enough to realize what had happened and to be absolutely convinced that I was going to die.

When I woke up on that hospital ship, even though I had nine tubes in me, my response on waking up was one of absolute ecstasy, joy, exhilaration. A couple of days later, the doctors came by and said, "We've got some good news and some bad news. The good news is that we're pretty sure you are going to live," and I laughed. I said, "I could have told you that as soon as I opened up my eyes." "The bad news is that you are going to paralyzed." And I remember saying, "Don't worry about it. That's O.K." I was so grateful to be given a second chance at life. In that moment of confronting my own mortality, all of what I had put my future in—business school, corporate America—evaporated. It just didn't seem to have the same meaning any more.

I came back and spent a year in Veterans Hospital, in New York City. My hospital was the basis of a scandalous exposé that was on network television, in newspapers, and in magazines; it portrayed the extraordinary conditions that at least some of us as returning veterans came back to. While the images could convey the overcrowding and the dilapidated facilities, they couldn't capture the despair in that institution. The fact that my closest friend, and ultimately eight of my friends with spinal cord injury, committed suicide was better testimony. I *had* to fight against that system, for reasons of my own survival. By going to a war that was extraordinarily brutal, and seeing death and experiencing almost dying, spending a year in a hospital that was so deplorable and despairing, that's what it took to take the athlete, the dutiful student, and transform him, for reasons of his own survival, to fighting against that system and to becoming an advocate.

Around that point President Nixon vetoed a Veterans Medical Care Expansion Act on the grounds that it was fiscally irresponsible and inflationary to provide adequate care to America's veterans. In the middle of that afternoon, I went to Times Square in Manhattan and blocked up traffic. I said, "Wait a minute. I was a marine infantry officer. I pulled in hundreds of thousands of dollars a day to kill people. I got shot, and now I come back and you tell me all of a sudden that it's fiscally irresponsible and inflationary to provide adequate medical care? I don't think so." I thought, "You know, I must be too stupid to know what my rights are."

So, I went to law school, got a law degree, but I found out that ain't the answer. What were needed were new laws. In an unbelievably naïve way, I figured that if somebody simply went to Washington and told the American people what was going on with Vietnam veterans, with this story being told, a compassionate and caring society would have to respond. Come on, this is basic stuff. After waiting a long time for somebody to do it, and nobody doing it, you finally get to the point when your attitude gets built up enough to say, "The hell with it—I'll do it!"

So, honest to God, a very unassuming guy simply went to Washington, D.C., with a hell of an attitude and started talking. I had the good fortune of having the editor of *The Washington Post* editorial page invite me into his office the second week I was there. He listened to the rap and said, "Hey, that's not bad." Next day, I had a full picture and a big *Washington Post* op-ed saying "Viet-

nam Veteran Advocate Arrives." It was the beginning of an extraordinary campaign of media. *The Washington Post* never undertook
an editorial campaign as they did for the next year on behalf of
what I was advocating. Never! *The New York Times* picked it up;
papers around the country picked it up. When *The New York Times*
covers you, you wind up going on ABC, CBS, NBC—network
television; you get a lot of amplification. Here's the bottom line,
and this is the point: I got a chance to tell my story! That story got
amplified and got shared with the American public. And guess
what? Not a single thing that we were fighting for was enacted
into law. That's a lesson. Simply to argue for something in terms
of justice, fairness, equity doesn't make it in our political process.
The members of Congress that came forward back then were guys
like Al Gore, Tom Daschle, Dave Bonior, Leon Panetta. Yeah,
give me those guys twenty years later, but back then, they were
freshmen! They didn't have any political strength.

The Veterans Committees in the House and Senate were controlled by guys that had been there for a lifetime! They had no
resonance with us, as the Vietnam generation. I remember going
into a congressional hearing one day about Vet Centers. *The New
York Times,* dutifully, had done an editorial that morning, arguing
the need for Vet Centers. The chairman of that committee holds
up that *Times* editorial and says, "You know, some people don't
get it. Where I come from"—which happened to be Mississippi—
"we don't run in harmony with *New York Times* editorials, we run
in opposition to that."

O.K. What we did is, we went grassroots. We went into the
districts from which the members of those committees were elected,
got onto their editorial pages, did their radio talk shows, and
brought the pressure not from the elite establishment but back
from within those districts. Finally, incrementally, we started to
bring on line the kinds of programs that were so critically needed
and deserved. We even got a measure of respect and recognition.

As part of the work with the Vietnam veterans, reconciliation with our former adversaries was an obvious, key part. In 1981, I had the privilege of leading the first group of veterans to go back to Vietnam; it was an extraordinary meeting, bringing about a whole process of reconciliation. That would be a whole other discussion, but, in short, we started humanitarian programs to try to connect the American people with the Vietnamese people. Also, since the big obstacle that stood between the United States and Vietnam was Vietnam's occupation of Cambodia, we went to Cambodia.

I will simply repeat what I said yesterday: it changed my life when I went to Cambodia more than the entire war experience in Vietnam, as brutal as that was, ever could, because what happened in Cambodia was genocide—and it is a whole different order of human experience. The horror that took place on the killing fields there is unimaginable. But Cambodia was unique in another way— that when you went to the capital city of Phnom Penh, you saw people hobbling all over the place. Amputees. You came to understand that there were more than five hundred people every single month getting blown up by landmines. There were more landmines in Cambodia than there were people. Cambodia was proportionately the most disabled society of any country in the world.

A couple of guys on our staff are themselves amputees as a result of landmines during Vietnam, and we said, "Look, this is nuts. Let's start a program and do some rehabilitative work with the amputees." Setting up a clinic, we went through a process of emotionally connecting with an issue that intellectually we understood was devastating. And I say we "emotionally" connected because the people that came into our clinics were people whose lives we came to understand and to touch. We realized that it was the poorest of the poor, the most vulnerable within the society, who were invariably winding up the victims of landmines. In the majority of cases, it wasn't even military people, but civilian. A couple of years back, a survey was done in Cambodia which showed that the leading cause of casualties was women going into the forest to gather firewood—wood is still the primary fuel. Also, it was the kids, either playing or bringing animals out to graze, that were getting blown up.

My God, what makes landmines different from all the other kinds of weapons that you could easily say we ought to get rid of? What makes landmines different is that they are totally indiscriminate. In the case of a machine gun, a rifle, an artillery piece, jet fire, whatever, you've got a target and you fire. There is a command and control function directing that fire. Landmines—there is none. You simply set it, you bury it, you hide it, and whoever happens to step on that landmine becomes the victim.

Now, after several years, we know that in probably over 80 percent of the cases, the people who wind up stepping on those landmines are innocent civilians, because, unlike basically all the other weapons, when the conflict ends, you put the rifles and the artillery pieces and the tanks and the helicopters back into the armories, but landmines stay out where you bury them—for years and years and years, doing exactly what they are designed to do, blowing off the leg of whoever it is that happens to step on it.

When I was on the hospital ship, the guys that cried the loudest were either burn victims or victims of landmines who suffered a traumatic amputation of a limb. When the dressing on that limb was changed, those guys would cry—literally, I swear, would cry—for their mothers. The guys who work in my office come in today and say, "Bobby, I didn't sleep last night. My foot was killing me." He doesn't have a foot; it's called phantom pains. Even though the body part is missing, you can still have extraordinary excruciating pains. And because of the nature of what happens with landmines, all this crap gets blown up your limb—shrapnel, dirt, garbage, clothing, etc.; you invariably go through a whole series of operations, where you are treated like a piece of salami; you keep getting resected and cut down. Other than burn cases, landmines cause the most debilitating, painful kind of injury that you could imagine. Understand that they are designed to do that: the amount of explosive charge is purposely limited so that when somebody gets blown up and they are lying on the ground, they wind up being a terribly demoralizing factor for those around them, and in addition they are a burden on the logistical process because they have to be medevacked.

You find out that landmines, in the millions in these countries, denied the land to people. You couldn't bring the refugees back from Thailand into Cambodia because the land was contaminated. "Oh my God," you start to realize, "this stupid three-dollar weapon winds up being the major destabilizing factor in these third world, agrarian-based societies that are trying to recover." You realize it's not just Cambodia—it's Afghanistan, Mozambique, Angola, Kurdistan, etc. Once you start to really understand this, you say, "Wait a second. This is a catastrophe!"

We came back and, having learned the lessons with the Vietnam vets that I discussed before, we didn't want freshmen members of Congress. We went to the most powerful guy that we could find. It's hard to believe that back in 1992 there were fifty-seven Democratic members in the Senate—fifty-seven Democrats. The guy that controlled the money on the Appropriations Committee was Senator Leahy. We said, "So long as you've got the strength, you're the committee chair, you control the bucks, we want you." Leahy, thank God—because of his having actually gone out of the country, unlike Jesse Helms, actually having gone to areas of conflict and having seen what landmines were doing to victims, said immediately, "I'll help you. But Bob, you gotta understand something: it's going to take years." I said, "Senator, that's O.K., we're going to stay with you," and he said, "Let me introduce the idea, because nobody is talking about landmines. Let me introduce it with a one-year moratorium just to get it on the boards, to get people to start thinking about it." And in 1992, the United States, believe it or not, unilaterally, was the first country to outlaw trafficking in antipersonnel landmines. Admittedly, Leahy used a little stealth maneuver and snuck it into law, but *we did it.*

I was with Leahy when he would talk about this with his colleagues; he would visualize these children in these areas of conflict and get tears in his eyes. This guy was passionate—he was committed. A year later when he went to the floor and said, "I want your support to extend this unilaterally-enacted moratorium for three more years," the Senate voted 100 to nothing to support that. I gotta tell you, the Senate doesn't vote 100 to nothing that the moon circles the earth, for God's sakes! This was extraordinary. That inspired the world. The fact that the United States actually was at the forefront of, at least, the rhetoric to get rid of landmines meant, "Hey, maybe there's an opportunity here." Other countries started to put together their efforts and said, "Let's go." Leahy banged our president, mercilessly, to keep it up. He would introduce legislation each year, ratcheting up the stakes on the landmine issue. He actually got our president to go the General Assembly of the United Nations and call on the world community to outlaw this weapon, to get rid of it.

The president's problem is that the world community listened to him and took him seriously, ultimately delivering an international agreement that, as you probably know, the United States didn't sign! You've got 133 countries out there that sign; we, who inspired this campaign, worldwide, and in many ways drove it, wound up at the last minute faltering and not doing it. Fair question: what's going on here? In '96 we took out a full-page *New York Times* open letter to the president: "Mr. President, getting rid of landmines is the militarily responsible thing to do." That was signed by General Norman Schwarzkopf, hero of the Gulf War; signed by General David Jones, former Chairman of our Joint Chiefs of Staff; signed by General Galvin, former NATO Supreme Allied Commander; signed by General Hollingsworth, who set up our defensive structures for Korea. Fifteen of the nation's most respected retired military leaders openly called on the president to get rid of this weapon. And I have to tell you, you should understand one thing: these guys are the ultimate American patriots. They would do nothing, *nothing*, to compromise the safety, the integrity, and the well-being of U.S. fighting forces anywhere in the world. The fact that they all leaned into this campaign and argued it should settle any concern that there is a real military issue involved.

The fact is, in Vietnam, landmines were the leading cause of casualties for our own forces. Also, for our peacekeepers through NATO and the U.N., it was the leading source of their casualties. U.S. soldiers would be better off if antipersonnel landmines were removed from the face of the earth. I went with several of the generals and got a chance to talk to the president, laid out all the arguments. His opponent back then, Bob Dole, supported us; Elizabeth Dole openly called for the abolition of the weapon. Not a member of Congress stood up and said we needed the weapon. The ICRC, known for its neutrality, was in the campaign, unprecedentedly so, to argue getting rid of it. They all recognized that it was a crisis.

"Mr. President, what more can we do?" *Quote: "You can get the Joint Chiefs off my ass. I can't afford a breach with the Joint Chiefs."* What made that comment remarkable is that standing next to me was the former *chairman* of the Joint Chiefs. He said, "Mr. President, that's why I am here. I and the other retired military officers will support you." *"I can't afford a breach with the Joint Chiefs."* We talk about democracy, civilian control of the military? The president listened to only one voice, the Joint Chiefs, which our military guys have made very clear are, institutionally, incapable of going to the commander-in-chief and suggesting that you take weapons out of their arsenal. That's not their job. It's the president's job, as the commander-in-chief, to balance off the ultimate humanitarian consequences with whatever marginal military value is there.

In our meetings over the last seven years with these guys over at the Pentagon, we've closed the door and asked, "Hey, what's going on here?" They've said, flat out, "This has nothing to do with antipersonnel landmines! They're garbage. The point is, we don't want to set a precedent, because if we let you reach into our arsenal and take out this weapon in large part because of its humanitarian consequences, then other categories of weapons and munitions systems, cluster bombs, etc., would be at risk." And that's where we stand today.

I want to summarize with a couple of simple, key points. The most significant lesson I have learned in my adult life is that things don't happen simply because they are right. You have to get political strength committed to what you are fighting for. And it is a fight. We've had the extraordinary fortune of having now a five-term Democratic senator go *nuts* on this issue and drive it for us. We had the Canadian foreign minister—Jody will be talking about him in a minute—who after years of work at the United Nations on that Convention on Conventional Weapons *failed*, because the United Nations is a consensus process and thus anyone around the table can block the process, but who, with great personal courage, said, "The hell with the United Nations. We are going to do something totally different. We are going to set a standard; we are going to invite anyone who wants to come and sign this treaty." When he did that, he got pounded; the U.S. went nuts, our allies berated him, but, at the end of the day, a year later, we got it.

So, individual leadership counts. Political strength has to be connected to the righteousness of your argument, and it's through life experiences that you come to have a role in determining how much you are going to get. A lot of the people here on this stage have been just like you; they went through changes that made them advocates, in response to injustices to which they were exposed. Each and every one of you can be up here in several years. And don't doubt that, please.

Thank you.

Discussion Among the Participants

Julian Bond: One hundred thirty-five countries signed the treaty; the U.S. did not. How can you hope for the treaty to have any effectiveness when the major power stands aloof?

Bobby Muller: The fact that so many countries have signed the treaty really puts pressure on the United States not to stand outside what is clearly the larger community of nations. The dynamic of having other countries challenge the United States by going forward, without it being a mutual deal, has been extraordinary. It is absolutely critical that we continue our efforts to get the United States to sign. One of the ironies is that we had a hell of a year last year; you wind up with a Diana who, through the tragedy of her death, connects this issue with the entire world. You get a Lloyd Axworthy who basically jettisons the existing mechanisms, breaks new ground and makes a treaty happen. You get the recognition of a Nobel Prize, and a lot of people think, "Hey, you guys did it! Congratulations. Next!"

They don't realize that this was a great step, but, my God, you've still got eighty to ninety million landmines in the ground, you've still got hundreds of thousands of victims, you have lots of critical countries that are not signatories. We are not, realistically speaking, going to universalize the support for this treaty by getting India, Pakistan, China, Russia, if we don't get the United States.

The ultimate effect of this effort is to stigmatize this weapon in the public's thinking such that anybody who does go ahead and use this weapon is branded a pariah, an outlaw. And that means that it has to be universally condemned. You cannot be looking to stigmatize this weapon if the world's superpower, the United States, which has every alternative capability to meet any possible military requirement, says, "It's O.K. to continue to use this weapon," because, in doing that, they undercut the moral imperative of the Ottawa Treaty, which says that this is an inhumane weapon that the world community cannot tolerate.

We have to put pressure on the U.S. Get them, get the others, truly universalize the support, and keep it what it needs to be: a humanitarian concern for people by doing the de-mining in all of the countries that need to be cleaned up and providing assistance to innocent victims around the world.

Julian Bond: President Arias Sánchez, how does this connect with the work that you do, that you are most identified with?

President Oscar Arias Sánchez: It is a source of inspiration. It teaches us that we must persevere. If it has taken them such a long time to bring this treaty with a minor, though very dangerous, weapon, how can we be hopeful if we are trying to regulate seven different categories of weapons that are all the weapons you can think of? If it has taken them six, seven years, perhaps it might take us twenty years, twenty-five years, thirty years, but at least it gives us a lot of hope—how an individual can make a difference.

Harn Yawnghwe: I know that you are working on this international treaty, but how does it, in a practical sense, affect areas of conflict? I know that a lot of countries haven't signed yet. For example, in Burma, the military is using landmines, and other groups are using them as well. How would you approach that process? It is going to be a big problem for us as well.

Bobby Muller: At the very beginning, somebody said to me, "The fact that you have outlaws is not a reason not to pass laws." The world is a better place because of the international agreements to prevent the use of poison gas, chemical and biological weapons, and the nuclear limitation agreements that we have, as with land-mines. None of these are the magic wand that's going to make it all better, but they do shift the baseline in the dynamics that underlie these concerns.

If we can effectively stop countries from manufacturing, exporting, and trafficking in the weapon, we are not going to have the situations that we had in the seventies and the eighties, in which major producer countries—which basically are signatories, or have at least acknowledged no further exports—fuel third-world conflicts by pouring millions and millions of landmines, like M&Ms, on top of other weapons into these areas. Some areas of the world are slower to bring on than other areas, but it's a process. The fact that the major producers are basically out of the business, certainly not selling and transporting, are major steps down the road that we have to continue to travel.

Jody Williams: I certainly agree with everything Bobby has just said. Part of the issue is that this is such a new norm. In one year's time, we achieved the Ban Treaty. It will take time to have that establishment of the norm solidified, but just the pressure that's been brought to bear by the political will of so many countries signing the treaty, so many countries ratifying it, has caused it to become binding international law on March 1, 1999, faster than any treaty in history. That pressure has made even countries that are still outside the process to take steps. China, for example, which has been one of the most vocal in opposition to a ban, has announced that they have stopped production for export as of 1996, and the United States, as Bobby mentioned, says they will sign now though we still need to work on them. When we were recently at the U.N. with Axworthy and others, talking about this issue, marking the fact that forty countries had ratified so it would enter into force, Foreign Minister Axworthy was able to tell us that he had just had a meeting with the foreign minister of China who, for the first time, announced that they are giving money to the trust fund for de-mining in Bosnia and that they are willing to commit de-mining expertise to train others. So, even though they are not as far as we would like them to be, just the fact that they are responding to the global awareness is very heartening. Additionally, our own military says that there have been no significant exports of antipersonnel landmines now for over four years.

I think the norm will be firmly established over time, and the public pressure and awareness have already made it increasingly difficult for countries to stay outside what is becoming increasingly accepted behavior. But, in order to avoid the Burmas of tomorrow from using mines, what we really need to do is to see the stockpiles destroyed. This treaty needs to enter into force as soon as possible so that the various timetables of the treaty start ticking. Countries that have ratified will have four years to destroy their stockpiles. You want the Angolas to sign and ratify and destroy. As they teeter on the brink of civil war again, it would certainly be less horrifying if they couldn't have the stocks of antipersonnel landmines to use in the ground again. Think of Cambodia. And also Kosovo, where they are using mines now. The faster we get this treaty really moving, the stocks destroyed, the sooner we have the possibility of diminishing the possibility of use in the future. So, it's part of a process, but we've accomplished a lot in a short period of time, and I am sure we will continue.

Dr. Rigoberta Menchú Tum: We have all admired this struggle and have united ourselves with it. As more people join this struggle, it has a bigger effect. I wanted to ask if there is a list of manufacturing companies that make landmines and if this information, this campaign, is getting to them. Usually, the manufacturer builds the bomb and it builds the thing that will dismantle it as well; it makes money on both ends. Thus I want to know more about this.

Bobby Muller: There have been many demonstrations at producers of landmines in this country. Human Rights Watch has put out reports on the producers, which are very detailed and are available if you simply call their offices. I think putting pressure at all points in the campaign makes an awful lot of sense.

People may not understand what we are talking about in demining. In '92, I went to the Pentagon and said, "O.K., how do we clean up all these landmines that are out there?" I was amazed when the Pentagon said, "We don't know." "What do you mean, you don't know?" And they said, "We don't know. We don't do that kind of work." They explained that the only concern they really had was looking at landmines as an obstacle in battle that had to be cut across. You can traverse a minefield in any one of many different ways. I'll give you one example. You can fire detcord—detonation cord—across the minefield, you blow it, and you are able to what they call "breach" the minefield. You may take a casualty, but it's combat, and that's what soldiers are designed, basically, to deal with.

The idea of actually lifting landmines out of an area was something that they had never put any energy into doing. They said, "Go talk to the humanitarians at the State Department." We go over to the State Department and say, "Hey, how do we do this?" They say, "What the hell are you doing here? That's a weapon. Go deal with the Pentagon." It is unbelievable, but as recently as 1992 we really didn't have any organized concepts of how to go about de-mining. Now we do. There are mechanisms, and more times than not, it is actually somebody with a very sensitive metal detector going over the ground, getting a signal, that digs up the landmine. The problem is that only one out of every 125 times the metal detector gets a signal that is actually a landmine. All the others times it's a piece of shrapnel, or sometimes even the ferrous content of the soil itself. But the point is: we now know that it can be done. It costs money to put these people in the field; it's slow, and it's dangerous, but it can be done. Countries have committed, pledged, millions of dollars, but the difference between the rhetoric and the reality is substantial, and we have to hold their feet to the fire to get the bucks actually committed. It's a problem that does have a solution, but it requires a commitment of political will to put the bucks up to get the job done.

Julian Bond: One other question about something you said a moment ago, about "magic wands." So many people, many of them young, seem to me to be suggesting that if we can't have magic wands that solve these problems [*snaps fingers*] like that, what's the use? What's the use in these long, protracted—the twenty or thirty years President Arias speaks of—what's the use? What's the use of these battles?

Bobby Muller: You gotta get smart. A good friend of mine, Tom Daschle, who is the minority leader in the Senate, said to me, "Bobby, you learned how to play the game. You take a very small piece of the action, and you stay focused on it for years. Just keep your focus, and slowly, incrementally, by sticking with it and maintaining a focus, you can get something done." I really believe that you gotta get into these efforts thinking in terms of decades. When we started this campaign, I had no doubt that we would get there. I thought it would take twenty years. I had no expectation that it would catch hold the way it did, but that's part of the play.

One of the things I have learned in Washington is KISS: Keep It Simple, Stupid. When you get something that you can explain in thirty seconds, you have a lot higher chance of success than something that needs a treatment of five minutes to lay out. The beauty about landmines is—I found out when we did telemarketing—guys could get on the phone and in thirty seconds get a commitment for bucks out of somebody on the other end. I said, "This is a good issue." The fact that it was simple and people could visualize it and the fact that it is a tragedy on the scale that it is, helped accelerate the time line. But if you want to do something serious, it's not going to happen—unless it's an extraordinary exception—on a short-time basis. In my book, you have to think at least ten years plus.

Jody Williams

United States

Short Biography

Jody Williams, the 1997 co-recipient of the Nobel Peace Prize, was born in Vermont in 1950. She learned to abhor injustice at an early age from fellow schoolchildren, who unfairly picked on her disabled brother. Like many teenagers of her generation, she also developed an aversion to the war then being waged in Vietnam.

After attending the University of Vermont in Burlington, Williams moved to Brattleboro, Vermont, where she earned a master's degree in teaching Spanish and English as a Second Language (ESL) from the School for International Training in 1976. She then taught ESL in Mexico for two years. It was her first exposure to extreme poverty.

From Mexico, she moved to Washington, D.C. There, she worked two jobs and attended the School of Advanced International Studies at The Johns Hopkins University, which led to a master's degree in international relations in 1984.

Enticed by a leaflet she had received on the street one day, Williams attended a meeting about human rights violations taking place in El Salvador. With her recent experiences in Mexico, she developed an immediate and passionate interest in U.S. policy toward Central America.

Transforming that passion into a career, she served from 1984 to 1986 as coordinator of the Nicaragua-Honduras Education Project, leading fact-finding delegations to the region. From 1986 to 1992, she also developed and directed humanitarian relief projects as the deputy director of the Los Angeles–based Medical Aid for El Salvador.

With the end of the Cold War, Williams began to consider another advocacy role. In a happy coincidence, Bobby Muller, president of the Vietnam Veterans of America Foundation, called Williams in late 1991 to see if she would be interested in coordinating a new initiative to ban landmines worldwide. After years of building public awareness about U.S. policy toward Central America, Williams leapt at the opportunity to mobilize foreign governments and non-governmental organizations in a common and worthwhile cause.

In October 1992, the International Campaign to Ban Landmines (ICBL) was formally launched by the VVAF, Handicap International, Human Rights Watch, medico international, Mines Advisory Group, and Physicians for Human Rights. These six groups, which became the original steering committee of the ICBL, issued a "Joint Call to Ban Antipersonnel Landmines" that included putting an end to the use, production, trade, and stockpiling of the weapon. They also urged governments to increase resources for humanitarian mine clearance and for victim assistance.

As the campaign's chief strategist, Williams wrote and spoke extensively on the landmine problem and the need for a total ban. Her audiences included the United Nations, the European Parliament, and the Organization of African Unity.

Together with Shawn Roberts, she co-authored *After the Guns Fall Silent: The Enduring Legacy of Landmines* (VVAF, 1995). Their book drew upon two years of field research in four mine-affected countries to detail the socio-economic consequences of landmine contamination. Besides the exorbitant medical costs of treating landmine victims, the long-term consequences to a community include reduced employment opportunities and lost access to land for agriculture, grazing, and trading.

"People have this idea that land-mined fields are set off with barbed wire like they are in World War II movies, but that's not how it is," Williams told a reporter for *Vogue* magazine. "They put them where people go. They put them next to watering holes, along the banks of the river, in the fields. It is not realistic for people to stay out of those areas."

Working without an office or staff, and relying primarily on fax machines and electronic mail to disseminate information, Williams ultimately convinced more than one thousand NGOs from sixty-plus countries to support the campaign. The ICBL gained tremendous visibility when Diana, the Princess of Wales, became a vocal landmine critic and visited landmine victims in Angola and Bosnia—two of the most heavily mined countries in the world—in the months before her death.

In October 1996 the Canadian government hosted a meeting of pro-ban governments. The participants had two goals: to formally signal their intention to ban landmines and to develop an "Agenda for Action," a step-by-step strategy for moving the ICBL forward. At the conclusion of that meeting, Lloyd Axworthy, the Canadian foreign minister, challenged the participants to return to Canada in one year to sign an international treaty banning landmines.

They rose to the challenge. In early 1997 Austria drafted a treaty and in September of that year, eighty-nine countries convened in Oslo, Norway, to negotiate the treaty's final language. A meeting was scheduled for December 4, 1997, at which the treaty would be signed by pro-ban governments in Ottawa, Canada.

In a little more than five years, Jody Williams and the ICBL had achieved their goal of raising public awareness about landmines and effecting a landmine ban. In recognition of their efforts, the Norwegian Nobel Committee named Williams and the ICBL as co-recipients of the 1997 Nobel Peace Prize.

In conferring the award to Williams and the ICBL, Francis Sejersted, chairman of the Norwegian Nobel Committee, said, "There are those among us who are unswerving in their faith that things can be done to make our world a better, safer, and more humane place and who also, even when the tasks appear overwhelming, have the courage to tackle them.... You have not only dared to tackle your task, but also proved that the impossible is possible. You have helped to rouse public opinion all over the world against the use of an arms technology that strikes quite randomly at the most innocent and most defenseless."

To date, more than 120 countries have ratified the landmine ban treaty. For her role in helping to make this happen, Williams has also received the 1998 Distinguished Peace Leadership Award from the Nuclear Age Peace Foundation, and the Fiat Lux Award from Clark University. She has been named a 1997 "Woman of the Year" by *Ms., Glamour,* and *Vanity Fair* magazines, and has received honorary doctorate degrees from Briar Cliff College, Marlboro College, the University of Vermont, and Williams College.

While she no longer works for the VVAF, Williams continues to assist the ICBL as its international ambassador.

JODY WILLIAMS
"International Organization in
the International Campaign to Ban Landmines"

I hope it seems that I've been paying attention to my esteemed colleagues, because I have learned a lot in these two days. Part of what fascinates me is common themes running through what we're all saying about our own contributions to the building of peace, which is a very long-term process. The one that's resonated most, which Bobby just said, is that most of us are just ordinary people. I remember Betty Williams starting her comments with "People considered me to be an ordinary housewife." Then she did go on to say, "What's an ordinary housewife?" But we are ordinary people.

Bobby, very powerfully, explained one part of the campaign. What I am going to do, briefly, is try to put it in the international context. I will explain how a bunch of ordinary people around the world came together to take the challenge of the U.S. president to eventually eliminate landmines and make it a reality. And also, in so doing, to create a new model of diplomacy in the post–Cold War world—one that threatens the status quo about how things are done and that makes smaller and mid-size countries working together with civil society a potential new superpower.

Ordinary citizens. Bobby powerfully told you what brought him and the Vietnam veterans to the conclusion that they had to go to the source of the problem and ban the weapon. I want to ask two of my colleagues to stand up. Steve Goose and Susan Walker, please stand up—more ordinary people who have come together to create extraordinary moments in history. Steve Goose works for Human Rights Watch, another founding member of the campaign. Human Rights Watch, in 1985, was the first organization to begin the systematic documentation of the impact of antipersonnel landmines—very important, when we went up against governments and militaries, to tell them that the weapon was already illegal, to explain to them the disproportionate consequences of its use on civilians. Without that documentation we would not have been able to argue with conviction. Susan Walker is currently one of the co-coordinators of this campaign. She works for the organization Handicap International, which works in thirty-nine countries around the world, putting limbs on mine victims—another organization that came to the belief that it had to join a political movement to ban this weapon because its consequences were too great. There were many like us around the world. It was the people in the field, the organizations doing the work in the middle of the minefields, who came to the conclusion that the cost of the use of this weapon—the cost to civilians—for decades after the end of the war, was so severe that it had to be outlawed. Many of them, like Handicap International, had never launched a campaign or participated in one. Human Rights Watch was great at documentation, but was not excited about coalition work and being political. Still, the consequences of this weapon were so grave that they believed it was time to take action.

It was these people with field expertise who came together, and, in 1992, we formally launched the International Campaign to Ban Landmines. Bobby described really well what happened in the United States. He clearly showed the early leadership of Senator Leahy in the United States, which galvanized much of the world. Both the campaign side, and governments, believed that if the United States—the sole remaining superpower—was willing, on its own, to stop the export of what was still considered to be a legal weapon, then maybe we could really do something. It made us all believe that maybe we could do something even if it might take two decades.

Our campaign started working at the international level and the national level. With our various national campaigns, as we grew, NGOs in the different countries—now 1,200 non-governmental organizations in seventy-five countries—formed in their own national campaigns, all of us united with the goal of banning the weapon. But the NGO in each campaign works independently because each society is different. Some are lobbyists; some are field workers. There was never an intention to dictate from the United States how our Mozambican colleagues, for example, were to approach their government, or how our colleagues in Cambodia were to approach their government. So, we each worked independently, but coordinating and communicating constantly toward a common goal.

On the international side, we challenged governments to come together to look at the one existing treaty, the Convention on Conventional Weapons—a product of the mid-seventies—a result, in part, of the Vietnam War. People had been horrified by the impact of landmines, napalm, and other such delightful weapons in the Vietnam War, and they came together, resulting in the Convention on Conventional Weapons. It was weak, it didn't do too much to stop the proliferation and use of landmines, but it was an existing vehicle that we could use as a focal point. We challenged governments to come together and amend it. We thought that if we pressed them enough, maybe we could get them to amend it—not to ban the weapon, because we knew there wasn't that much political will yet, but at least we could get some movement. We achieved that very rapidly.

Then, as the national campaigns developed their own relationships with their respective political people, we caused governments to begin to recognize that this was an issue that was growing in concern around the world. Governments wanted to be seen as the good guy in this issue, and they began to compete for leadership on this issue of global, humanitarian concern. Governments have egos just like individuals. Obviously, they are more complex egos, but they do have egos. When Leahy shocked the world with the moratorium on export, it incensed the French, for example. Considering themselves to be the guardians of human rights, they immediately responded to the challenge and launched their own moratorium. Then we were able to get our campaigns, for example, in Germany, to say, "O.K., France has done it, the U.S. has done it, why can't you do it?" Then, Denmark, and then Norway, and we kept building and building, and finally we got one country to unilaterally ban completely the use, production, trade, and stockpiling of antipersonnel landmines: Belgium, in March of 1995, the new leader. It was amazing. Then Austria did the same thing. Then the Netherlands. All the while, the United States still claimed leadership as the other countries of the world moved forward, becoming the new leaders.

Words are cheap. "Tears," as Betty said, "without action are irrelevant." The words of leadership became hollow when other countries took the real lead by action. I can say I'm going to do a million things, but it's what I do that matters. Unfortunately, leadership remained on the Hill and not in the rest of the administration in this country. But because other countries were willing to do it differently, because they were willing to show leadership, a novel thing happened: we were developing a new partnership between governments and non-governmental organizations in the areas of arms control, disarmament, and humanitarian law. Governments are relatively comfortable with civil society talking about tear-jerking issues like children, tear-jerking issues like women, trees, the environment. Right? "These are soft and easy issues, and you guys can talk about 'em, but in the manly issues of war and peace and armament, tree-hugging liberals have no place."

Because we were the experts from the field, the experts with the documentation, we knew what we were talking about, and they could not disregard us. We were always there, dialoguing with them, pushing them, proving time and time again that what we said was right and doing everything we said we would do. The most important thing, in many instances in the campaign, was follow-up. Every time we said, "We are going to X, Y, or Z," we did it. Whether it was with our campaign colleagues or it was governments, we did it, did it, did it. That builds trust. You do what you say you are going to do, so people know that when you say it, you mean it. When this campaign said it, it meant it, and we proved it. This broke through, a little bit, the barriers of distrust between government and civil society—distrust which is so odd because we elect governments and they should be open to what we have to say, but they are not, generally, especially on issues of arms control and laws of war.

We were able to build that trust to such a degree that we worked very closely with the Canadians in paving the groundwork for the tremendous leadership of Lloyd Axworthy when, in October of 1996, he challenged the world. We had been in a three-day meeting, there were fifty governments that called themselves "pro-ban." The campaign had worked hard to set up an agenda for action which might ultimately lead to the eventual elimination of landmines. As Bobby said, the U.S. thought they would run the show, in normal diplomatic channels, and it would happen in twenty years—maybe. At the end of three difficult days of very difficult work, because we actually made the diplomats work, which is unusual in a conference, Lloyd Axworthy stood up to give the closing address and to congratulate everybody, as politicians are expected to do. "Thank you all for coming, and thank you for this wonderful action plan. Now we have maybe a road map"—then he paused and said, "But this road map is not enough. It is no longer enough to say that we are *eventually* going to eliminate antipersonnel landmines. We have been hearing that now for years. The Canadian government challenges you to come back in one year's time, having negotiated a total ban on the use, production, trade, and stockpiling of antipersonnel landmines based on this Austrian Draft Treaty. Canada is so determined to set a new international norm that even if we are sitting here alone with the International Campaign next year, we are going to sign this treaty to prove that at least one government—or two or ten—are committed to setting a new norm to get rid of this horrific weapon."

That freaked out the diplomats horribly, because the Canadians had not consulted with anyone—they hadn't consulted with the other leaders like Belgium, Austria, the Netherlands. Normally, you chat with your colleagues, discussing whether or not this is a good thing to do. The Canadians knew that if they chatted with their colleagues they would have been shot down and nothing would happen, so they just did it. Then, to further horrify the diplomatic community, they said, "Not only are we going to do this, we will do it in open, complete partnership with the International Campaign to Ban Landmines, and they will be inside the negotiations. They are going to hear you when you negotiate." He didn't say these words, but the implication was: "You won't be able to stand outside the negotiating doors and pretend you're doing the right thing but then go inside, shut the doors, and keep civil society out—the same civil society without which this never would have happened—and non-negotiate the ban." So we were in the room.

That is leadership. That is huge risk-taking. It was such a huge risk that it almost collapsed. Canada so enraged its partners in the ban movement by grandstanding, by taking the lead, that they could have lost their allies, but, again, they put action behind their words. They didn't just sit back and let it collapse. They went out and lobbied and pushed and put their money where their mouth was, and *made them stay.* When we went to negotiations, since the most mined countries in the world are the developing world, Canada paid to bring those diplomats to every single negotiating session so they were part of the treaty. That *never* happens. Treaties are negotiated in Geneva, where the rich countries have their missions; they send their people who are always stationed in Geneva at the mission. The developing world does not have enough money to be there, so they're not involved, but then, they are expected to become party to something that they had nothing to do with. Canada said, "Nuh-uh, not this one. These are the guys that are living with the landmines, they are going to be with us." And they were at every meeting; we even held meetings in Africa to make sure.

When the world came together a year later to sign the treaty, there were 122 governments that signed in two days. It was incredible! Despite the opposition of the United States, despite end-runs by the U.S. during the negotiations to derail it, the commitment was there—it had been publicly made, we were there with them—and they could not turn back. So we achieved a total-ban treaty in one year—five years, as Bobby says, from the launch of the campaign. It is for this that the campaign received the Nobel Peace Prize.

The first words of the announcement were "For making a utopian dream"—we were called "utopian" in the early days. It's absurd. Militaries have had these weapons since the U.S. Civil War, since the Crimean War; every single military in the world has this weapon. *"Do you think you are going to get them to give it up? The military has never met a weapon it doesn't like. You are utopian fools."* Well, we took this utopian dream of ordinary fools and made it a reality.

The other reason that the Nobel Committee chose to recognize the work of the International Campaign was the new model in the post–Cold War period, this model being civil society working with smaller and mid-size governments to bring about rapid change in critical issues of concern to the international community. They said that they hoped this model would be used over and over to deal with critical issues of arms control and peace in the next century.

For those of us who have worked diligently on this campaign, the treaty was the first step; there's an awful lot of work to be done. It's critical that this treaty succeed. As I mentioned, it will become international law more quickly than any treaty ever in history. The campaign is working to monitor the implementation by governments in a project called "Landmine Monitor" to make sure the governments do what they say they are going to do. Just as we did to get them to make the treaty, we are doing the same to make sure they obey their own treaty. *Impunity.* We do not want to create another piece of paper that is not adhered to and thus fosters the increasing sense of impunity in this world. If those governments come together and create this law themselves, and they sign and they ratify, they will adhere, because we will be there making sure that they adhere. Impunity is a horrific problem, obviously, and we do not want to contribute to impunity. So, we are committed to continuing our work for the treaty itself, and equally for the model.

Diplomats around the world are concerned that this model has succeeded. It disrupts the way things are done. It disrupts their process, it disrupts their job, it disrupts the way governments do things. If we succeed, and others are able to use this model, it is threatening to their whole process. Others are already trying to use this model. The International Criminal Court was another major example of the U.S. not understanding that in the post–Cold War period, civil society and governments are coming together to do it differently. The U.S. tried to get its interests inserted into the International Criminal Court at the cost of everybody else's beliefs, and the world said, "No." First the Ban Treaty and then the International Criminal Court. People are now trying to do it to stop child soldiers. The U.S. is against that.

People are also trying to limit light arms and small weapons. We were with President Arias and José Ramos-Horta in Belgium a couple of weeks ago on a very interesting initiative, trying to use parts of our campaign that were successful. President Arias' Code of Conduct is a harder job—seven categories of weapons. But I believe that if the model we've developed is applied, forcing governments to continue to accept us as partners, we will succeed, but if we step back and let it become business as usual, diplomacy as usual, power-politics as usual, it will be sentiment without action, which is irrelevant to changing the world.

We didn't set out to change the world. *We were ordinary people who saw a problem and believed we could do something to make it*

better. We never expected that we'd be sitting here with these eminent people because of what we did. We saw a problem, we knew
it had to be resolved, we came together to do it. Action, not crying.
It was ordinary people who have achieved an extraordinary thing
and given activists all over the world the belief that activists anywhere can and do make a difference. So don't sit back and worry,
don't sit back and cry, and don't sit back and wait for the other
guy to make it better. Join in, and help make it better yourself.

Thank you.

Discussion Among the Participants

Julian Bond: One thing that struck me about your description of
the campaign is the pulling together of this coalition of many
different organizations, not all of which are prepared to do the
same thing at the same time in the same way. I imagine that's a
difficult process for each of the people sitting around the table.
Tell us a bit about how it was done; how did you do it?

Jody Williams: The idea of dealing with the problem of landmines is not new. As I mentioned earlier, people were trying to
deal with the problem of indiscriminate and excessively injurious
weapons as a result of the Vietnam War in the mid-seventies. There
were initial steps then, but it wasn't until the end of the Cold War,
when people were no longer totally obsessed with the possibility
of complete nuclear destruction, that we started to look at how
wars had actually been fought on the ground—the weapons that
had been used and the impact of those weapons.

By the end of the Cold War and the collapse of the Soviet Union,
there were lots of groups in the world working in heavily mined
countries where previously they had not had access—such as Afghanistan, Cambodia, Angola, and Mozambique, as democracy
was emerging in these countries, and they saw the amazing devastation of landmines. Not just the immediate devastation of the
victims, but the devastation caused by the presence of millions of

landmines. Cambodia has millions of landmines scattered throughout 50 percent of its national territory. How do you repatriate refugees to create a new life when *half* of your national territory is full of landmines? Laos is full of unexploded munitions from the Vietnam War. A variety of concerned organizations were starting to talk about the situation. Field people would send reports back to Handicap International. They kept saying, "God, everywhere we go, we have mine victims, mine victims. We can't just keep putting limbs on them, we have to take political action." A group in Australia in 1992 got 2,500 people to petition the Australian government to try to do something about landmines. People were starting to deal with the crisis. Also, Human Rights Watch and Physicians for Human Rights had done fabulous work to stop the coward's war—landmines in Cambodia. They called for a ban. Prince Sihanouk spoke at the U.N., calling for a ban. People began really to recognize that action was needed, and it just took a couple of organizations—Bobby Muller at VVAF and medico international of Germany—to say "O.K., there seems to be something going on here; let's bring it together and create a political movement." The only thing that joined us was the common goal of banning the weapon. Every organization that joined then or joins now is free to do whatever they want to contribute to that process. In this way, the movement doesn't impinge on their own mandate, it doesn't try to dictate to them the form they should take, but because there is the freedom to do it the way they want, they voluntarily come together.

And every time we have a meeting, we develop an action plan. This campaign has never had a "talking head" meeting, ever. Every single campaign meeting, whether it's been 450 people from fifty countries in Mozambique during the Ottawa process, or seventy people in London in May of 1993, we came out with an action plan so that our people knew what to do next. They could choose to either do it in a big way or in a little way, but we always were clear about the next steps. It's a combination of letting them be free and giving them a little guidance.

Bobby Muller: Can I give a reinforcing comment there? It was just a year ago when the Nobel Committee called. I'll certainly never forget that morning. This guy Geir Lundestad called, and he said, "Ah, congratulations, Mr. Muller. The International Campaign to Ban Landmines has been awarded the Nobel Peace Prize, along with Jody Williams." And I said, "Oh, that's great Mr. Lundestad, but we've got a problem." "Oh, what's that?" I said, "Well, there really isn't an International Campaign to Ban Landmines." My generational marker is "follow the money"—you remember the old Woodward-Bernstein "Deep Throat?" "There's a check. There's no entity to give a check to," I said. "The International Campaign to Ban Landmines is a name given to the collective action of a lot of organizations. It doesn't exist as an organization. There is no president, vice president, secretary, treasurer; there's no board of directors. We never had budget meetings. So, what are ya gonna do?" It turned out to be quite a dilemma—but that's another story! But I think the idea of setting a goal line and saying, "Look, all of you out there, in whatever way you can—if you agree that this is a deserving goal line to cross—you are a supporter of the campaign; do whatever you can in your community, in your country, to collaboratively support this collective effort to move it downfield." In that sense, I think this is a refreshing way of organizing a movement compared to what a lot of us have struggled through in collaborative efforts.

Julian Bond: Perhaps that is the secret of your success.

Jody Williams: I would stress what I said at the podium: follow up. Follow up, follow up, follow up. People so often ask, "God, how could you organize all this?" It's drudgery. The real nuts-and-bolts work of this campaign is drudgery. It was getting up at 3:30 in the morning, every day, and faxing people all over the world to say, "This is what the French accomplished today. When you meet with your government, use it. Even though everybody was independent to do it their own way, they cared enough to keep us all informed so that we all had the power of the smoke-and-mirrors illusion of this huge machinery. It was the information. It was the information. We got so good at the information that governments called us, rather than other governments, to find out what was happening next, because we usually knew before they did. It was, again, the follow up, the constant communication, the building of trust. Trust, trust, trust—*the* most important element in political work. Once you blow trust, you've blown it all. It's hard to rebuild. Just as in relationships. You do what you say you're going to do. And if you say you're going to do something, and you don't do anything.... Sentiment without action is irrelevant.

His Holiness the Dalai Lama: Is there any possibility that, like what you have done, someone could start a movement to ban nuclear weapons?

Jody Williams: It is certainly a different issue. If a country gives up antipersonnel landmines, it doesn't put its entire existence at threat. A handful of nations that have nuclear weapons still have the mentality that, if they give them up, they're putting themselves at risk, threatening their entire existence. However, I am increasingly of the belief that more could be done now in the post–Cold War period. Part of it was the nuclear standoff between the two blocs of power. I am not unconvinced that if there were a new approach in this new period, more concerted than before, something might be done. It wouldn't be as quick as landmines.

Bobby Muller: Leadership counts. Having people come to the fore and be the catalytic agent, and spark movements, counts. In that sense, I am inspired by what I am seeing happening right now. The person who was the commanding general for all the United States' nuclear capabilities, General Lee Butler, has, just within the last year, spoken out—on the basis of his career and his responsibilities in dispatching America's nuclear capabilities—to advocate the abolition of nuclear weapons. When he was in charge of nuclear weapons, he went over to the then–Soviet Union and met his counterpart, and they got to be good friends. His counterpart, who shares a lot of his beliefs, is now the minister of defense within Russia. There are very serious negotiations going on right now about not only the reduction, but working towards the elimination, of nuclear weapons.

Bringing the retired military leadership that we were able to recruit into the Landmine Campaign was an extraordinary factor in undercutting the military's opposition to this campaign. When some of their most illustrious and reputable leaders joined our side, when you have somebody who is a four-star retired general officer, who had for years been responsible for the dispatch of our entire nuclear capability, saying, "You unleash forces which are too dangerous to unleash. You run risks which are too great to tolerate. We have to walk the nuclear cat back," that is a powerful spark for this movement. I think that kind of leadership and the dynamic of what is going on around the world community, including the inability of the Russians to manage their nuclear arsenal, provide extraordinary opportunities that, hopefully, we will see this movement on.

Questions from the Audience

Jeffrey Hopkins: The first question is in the same line, and it is for President Arias. Landmines and nuclear weapons share many similarities, especially their indiscriminate destruction of civilians. Therefore, can a non-governmental campaign be effective in ending the use of nuclear weapons?

President Oscar Arias Sánchez: Yes, I believe so. It is obvious; civil society is becoming more and more important every day. Civil society is far ahead of governments in pushing issues. This has been shown in Rio, in the case of the environment. This has been shown in Cairo, in Beijing with women's issues, etc. What we need is commitment, political will, leadership, and, as it has been said, "Words are cheap; tears without actions are irrelevant."

I know General Lee Butler; I think this is wonderful. His is the minority view, however, in this country, as it is the minority view concerning the seven categories of the International Code of Conduct on Arms Transfers. We are dealing here with the most powerful interest groups on earth, much more powerful than the tobacco industry, than the pharmaceutical industry, whatever you can think of. As I said before, it is not jobs that are behind the sale of weapons, it is profits. It is a very strong force against peace and humanity. But action is what is needed. If we all become activists, perhaps this goal of controlling weapons or destroying nuclear arsenals could become a reality, and the dream could come true in twenty years' time, thirty years' time. It is a great challenge for future generations—to have ideals, to understand that the idealists of today are the realists of tomorrow and that tears become irrelevant if there is no action and commitment.

Jeffrey Hopkins: The next question is for Betty Williams. Yesterday, several of you brought up how emotion without action is nothing. So, how can I, as a college student with very little money, move beyond being emotional about people, justice, and reconciliation, and act in such a way that will help to make a difference?

Betty Williams: I'd like to quote for you now one of my favorite people in the whole world. She's an anthropologist named Margaret Mead. "Never doubt that a committed group of people, however small they may be, can change the world. In fact, it is the only thing that ever has." Being afraid of just being the one person to take the step will keep you forever from taking the step. I stay out there, even when I get a punch in the jaw, which happens quite frequently.

I'll get knocked over. You know that song "I Get Knocked Down, But I Get Up Again"? Well, that happens to me at least forty times a week. Boom, boom, boom. This work is like that. We have to know, too, that there are no quick fixes. Our world did not get into this condition overnight. We, as human beings, are not capable of pulling it out of this condition overnight. It's going to take hard work, dedication, courage, and commitment to do it.

Over lunch today, I was asked a question about the peace movement in Northern Ireland. Mairead and I thought it would take fifty years, at least, to deal with three hundred years of bad history. It took much less than that. But, if you go out there and think you're going to have an immediate solution then you're absolutely crazy. The campaign that I am running to create safe havens for children—I know that I may never see success in my lifetime—and that's O.K. because if I do the job right, the job goes on when I'm not here. Each one of us at this table would feel that we all would love to see a non-violent, beautiful, just, and peaceful world, but until we are willing to work for it, as individuals and not just people sitting around a table, it's never going to happen. So, don't be afraid, and don't think that your voice doesn't make a difference. Your voice makes a huge difference.

Jeffrey Hopkins: The next question is for Dr. Menchú Tum. What place has prayer in achieving individual and world peace?

Dr. Rigoberta Menchú Tum: I think it is very important to pray for peace, but to pray for peace just to pray for peace really doesn't contribute very much. Prayer and action are both things that are important together. Also, an individual struggle for peace has many limits; it is a lot better to struggle together with others—especially with people who have a great desire and need for peace, and especially to work with those people who also have a proposal about what to do for the future, because a lot of people struggle for peace just to get a title and an award. It may very well be that he or she will get the award but nothing changes, and it may very well be that she or he will be waiting and waiting for the award and it never arrives. It is more than a struggle of individuals; it is a struggle of peoples, of citizens, of young people and of old people, and of institutions of educators. I sometimes pray an Our Father for humanity, but it is the easiest thing that one can do.

Jeffrey Hopkins: The next question is for Bobby Muller. What is your position on the new landmines, which can be deactivated when the military action is finished?

Bobby Muller: The military has tried to argue that, since we have the technology and the money for this new generation of landmines—which will, after a certain period of time, blow themselves up or, if they malfunction and don't blow themselves up, they will essentially run themselves down so that they will be neutralized and will not represent a continuing humanitarian threat around the world—we should be allowed to keep our landmines. Well, think about it; this is International Diplomacy 101; you're sitting at a table, you've got representatives of ninety countries there—and the United States actually tried to present that position: "Since we have the money and technology for this new generation of landmines, we want all of you out there to give up your landmines. We're going to keep ours, and if you want, you can buy them from us." It didn't go very well. It's obvious that if we want everybody out there to get rid of their landmines, we have to give up our landmines.

Jeffrey Hopkins: The final question is for Jody Williams. About the Landmine Campaign, where do students, who are people at a relatively young and green age, fit in? How can we help?

Jody Williams: You could join the U.S. Campaign to Ban Landmines. That would be a good start. As Bobby has made very clear, there's still a lot of work to be done. It's coordinated out of Vietnam

Veterans in Washington. Start a student chapter. Take leadership here. Educate people here. Invite speakers on the issue here. Write to the President. Write to your representative. Write to the Joint Chiefs of Staff in particular—they're not used to getting fan mail.

His Holiness the Dalai Lama

Tibet

Short Biography

Many people embrace a faith that advocates non-violence. Yet few have been so tested in their beliefs as Tenzin Gyatso, His Holiness the 14th Dalai Lama of Tibet. As the spiritual and temporal leader of Tibet, the Dalai Lama (meaning "Ocean of Wisdom") has consistently opposed the use of force against the Communist Chinese who invaded his homeland in 1950. Instead, for almost fifty years, he has steadfastly proposed peaceful solutions and compromises based on mutual tolerance and respect for all people, including adversaries.

"At the heart of Buddhist philosophy is the notion of compassion for others," the Dalai Lama has said. "It should be noted that the compassion encouraged by Buddhism is not the usual love one has for friends or family. The love being advocated here is the kind one can have even for another who has done one harm."

At issue is whether Tibet is an independent nation. Tibetans cite almost two thousand years of self-governance as evidence of their sovereignty. The Chinese cite two historic incidents—a marriage between a Tibetan king and a Chinese princess in 641 (the king actually had five wives, including three Tibetan and one Nepalese) and a peace pledge signed by the two countries in 821—as "proof" that Tibet is part of China.

Few would disagree that the Chinese occupation of Tibet has been harmful. As early as 1960, the International Commission of Jurists reported that the People's Republic of China had violated sixteen articles of the Universal Declaration of Human Rights in Tibet and that they were guilty of "the most pernicious crime that any individual or nation can be accused of, viz. a willful attempt to annihilate an entire people."

Since the occupation began, the Chinese have directly or indirectly caused the deaths of more than 1.5 million Tibetans. They have transferred more than 7 million ethnic Chinese into Tibet, making Tibetans minorities in their own country and causing shortages in land and food. China has built nuclear missile sites on Tibetan soil and uses the country as its nuclear waste dumping ground. It is aggressively clear-cutting forests for lumber, which has led to serious erosion and flooding problems, especially in neighboring India and Nepal but also in China.

Even worse for the unique Tibetan culture, the Chinese have forcibly suppressed Buddhism—the backbone of this historically religious country. This suppression has resulted in the destruction of 6,000 Buddhist monasteries and shrines. Buddhist monks and nuns have been arbitrarily executed, imprisoned, or detained. Rare Buddhist manuscripts and artifacts have either been destroyed or sold. Images of the Dalai Lama, whom Tibetan Buddhists believe to be an incarnation of compassion, have been banned.

The Dalai Lama has tried to negotiate a resolution since 1950, when at age sixteen he assumed full political leadership of Tibet. His efforts included traveling to Beijing in 1954, where he talked to Mao Zedong, Zhou Enlai, Deng Xiaopeng, and other Chinese leaders, and to India in 1956, where he met with India's Prime Minister Nehru.

In 1959 rumors of his intended murder or kidnapping by the Chinese military forced the Dalai Lama to flee to India. There, in Dharamsala, he set up the Tibetan Government-in-Exile, through which he appealed to the United Nations for help. In response, the U.N. adopted three separate resolutions urging China to respect the human rights of Tibetans and their desire for self-determination. In 1963, the Dalai Lama promulgated a democratic constitution for Tibet.

In 1987 he proposed a Five-Point Peace Plan at a Congressional Human Rights Caucus in Washington, D.C. This plan called for making Tibet an international peace zone and environmental preserve—"a sanctuary of peace and nonviolence," he said, "where human beings and nature can live in peace and harmony." The plan also called for ending the transfer of ethnic Chinese into Tibet, restoring basic human rights and democratic freedoms to Tibetans, abandoning Chinese nuclear weapons production and waste dumping in Tibet, and beginning "earnest negotiations" to resolve the issue. A year later, he amended his Peace Plan before the European Parliament in Strasbourg, France, by stating that he would agree to the creation of a self-governing, democratic Tibet that functioned "in association with the People's Republic of China."

These efforts, while as yet unsuccessful in achieving a resolution, earned the Dalai Lama the 1989 Nobel Peace Prize. In presenting the award, Egil Aarvik, chairman of the Norwegian Nobel Committee, said that the Dalai Lama's "policy of non-violence is all the more remarkable when it is considered in relation to the sufferings inflicted on the Tibetan people during the occupation of their country.

"The Dalai Lama's response has been to propose a peaceful solution which would go a long way to satisfying Chinese interests. It would be difficult to cite any historical example of a minority's struggle to secure its rights, in which a more conciliatory attitude to the adversary has been adopted than in the case of the Dalai Lama."

Since winning the Nobel Peace Prize, the Dalai Lama has signed the 1991 Universal Declaration of Nonviolence and received other peace awards for his continuing advocacy in that area. A distinguished scholar of Buddhist philosophy, he has received several honorary doctorate degrees from Western universities. He is the author of several books, including *Kindness, Clarity, and Insight* and *Ethics for the New Millennium.*

His decades-long labors on behalf of Tibet may yet bear fruit. In June 1998, following talks with U.S. President Bill Clinton, Chinese President Jiang Zemin agreed to open up discussions with the Dalai Lama on Tibet's status.

In the meantime, the Dalai Lama travels throughout the world seeking support for Tibet, as well as promoting global environmental causes and advocating that all beings take responsibility for each other.

"Today the world is smaller and more interdependent," he has said. "Thus, without a sense of universal responsibility, our very survival becomes threatened. Basically, universal responsibility is feeling for other people's suffering just as we feel our own. It is the realization that even our enemy is entirely motivated by the quest for happiness. We must recognize that all beings want the same thing that we want. This is the way to achieve a true understanding, unfettered by artificial consideration."

HIS HOLINESS THE DALAI LAMA
"The Need for Compassion in Society: The Case of Tibet"

My English is very poor, and also my English is getting older, so it is difficult to express myself fully. I am extremely happy and privileged to participate in this gathering. I have learned some new things and also got some kind of feeling, more convincing, that if ordinary people see their objective clearly, then once determined, they can change things. That is a great inspiration. Also, I really admire some of these detailed presentations, like that of the former president of Costa Rica—wonderful, wonderful. All the presentations were very impressive.

Now, my own presentation: compassion in society and the case of Tibet. I believe that in human actions, the prime mover is motivation. On the spot, it is important to tackle the symptoms of problems, but in the long run, it is necessary to look at the motivation and whether there is a possibility to change it. For the long run, this is crucial. As long as the negative motivation is not changed, then although there might be certain rules and methods to stop counterproductive actions, human beings have the ability through various ways to express their negative feeling. Thus, for the long run, we need to look at our motivation and try to change it. This means that we must try to cultivate the right kind of motivation and try to reduce the negative motivation.

Basically, the concept of "I" is key. The things that surround you, all these ultimately are designated, so the designator, the self, is supreme. That's why, in many countries, one's own country is the center of the universe. Then, within the country, ultimately the person himself or herself is the center of the whole universe. Now, this self wants happiness and does not want suffering. Generally speaking, violence produces suffering; compassion or non-violence brings us happiness. Therefore, violence we consider to be negative, and non-violence we consider to be positive. Violent things like Hurricane Mitch in Central America are without any motivation, so we call them natural disasters. These we can't avoid. But in the other type of violence, which is created by humans ourselves, motivation is involved. Those kinds of violence can be changed—we can reduce them, and there is even a possibility to eliminate them. Therefore, we need to try to change our attitude, to cultivate the right kind of motivation.

Through what methods? I feel that prayer or religious belief is to some extent useful and can be helpful. But basically, simple awareness—knowledge of long-term and short-term consequences—

brings great help. If we make clear to people the negative long-term consequences, eventually they can develop clear realization that these negative, violent activities are bad, because of inducing painful experience and unhappiness.

Again, what is violence and non-violence? We can't make a clear demarcation between violence and non-violence on a superficial basis, since it is related with motivation. Out of sincere motivation, certain verbal actions, as well as physical actions, may *look* more wrathful, more violent, harsher, but in essence, because these activities come out of a sincere motivation of compassion, or a sense of caring, they are essentially non-violent. On the other hand, with negative motivation, trying to cheat, trying to exploit, trying to deceive, and using nice words—although with a big artificial smile and with a gift—might look like a friendly gesture, but because of the motivation, it is the *worst* kind of violence. So I feel that in certain cases violence can be said to be a manifestation or expression of compassion. Nevertheless, non-violence is the basic expression of compassion; therefore, the concepts of non-violence and compassion are very, very close.

In order to promote non-violence and reduce violence, ultimately we have to address motivation through education, through awareness. Here, I want to share with you a few thoughts about the concept of war. In ancient times, when people remained separately, more or less independently, there was no need for other people's cooperation. You could survive, you could live, completely independently. Under those circumstances, the concept of war, destruction of your enemy, and the victory of your side were a real possibility. Today's world is no longer that kind of reality. Your survival, your success, your progress, are very much related with others' well being. Therefore, under these circumstances even your enemies—for whatever reason you categorize them as an enemy in the economic field and in some other fields—and you are still very much interdependent. In such a situation, destruction of your enemy is actually destruction of yourself. Judging from that view-point, the concept of "we" and "they" no longer applies. Thus the concept of war, destruction of the other side, is not relevant to today's situation. Therefore, I think it is very important to make it clear that the concept of war not only is a painful experience but also is self-destructive.

Non-violence and peace do not mean that we remain indifferent, passive. Problems and contradictions always remain. I believe that as long as human beings remain, as long as human intelligence is present, some kind of conflict, some kind of contradiction, always remains. If we look at contradictory or different ideas, they are not necessarily negative. Even if we consider our body, many elements co-exist. These elements oppose one another—they are contradictory. Forces that contradict one another are the basis of further development; things stay more balanced, and that is healthy. Therefore, as long as this smart human brain remains, some kind of contradiction is always there. Even within one single person—because of the power of imagination, the power of vision, you get different ideas: in the morning, something different, and in the evening, something different. There are big differences, contradictions. Sometimes these are so great that, if one lacks the ability to overcome them, even suicide sometimes can occur.

We need a method, a technique, to overcome these contradictions. That is compromise. In today's reality the only way to solve a problem is compromise. Since your interest is very much related with others' interests, you can't sacrifice others' interests. Therefore compromise, 50-50. Realistically speaking, there is no possibility of 100 percent victory for oneself. If possible, one's own side 60 percent, other side 40 percent! If possible, that's the best!

But while reality is much changed, our perception, our way of thinking, remains behind. We retain an attitude that is essentially outmoded—"my nation," "their nation," "my religion," "another's religion," and sometimes the beautiful name "patriotism" is used with too much narrow-minded nationalism, sometimes even making people mad.

Since the situation in which we live is much changed but the attitude of the people who are in that situation is at variance with the times, this is one of the causes of unnecessary pain, unnecessary problems. Therefore, education is needed to communicate that the concept of violence is counterproductive, that it is not a realistic way to solve problems, and that compromise is the only realistic way to solve problems. Right from the beginning, we have to make this reality clear to a child's mind—the new generation. In this way, the whole attitude towards oneself, towards the world, towards others, can become more healthy. I usually call this "inner disarmament." Without inner disarmament, it is very difficult to achieve genuine, lasting world peace.

So, it is extremely important to look inward and try to promote the right kind of attitude, which is based on awareness of reality. A sense of caring for others is crucial. And it is actually the best way of caring for oneself. Because human nature is social, in simple things we need human companions with a genuine human smile. That provides us comfort, satisfaction. As I mentioned yesterday, the moment you think of others, this automatically opens our inner door—you can communicate with other people easily, without any difficulties. The moment you think just of yourself and disregard others, then because of your own attitude, you also get the feeling that other people also have a similar attitude toward you. That brings suspicion, fear. Result? You yourself lose inner calmness. Therefore, I usually say that although a certain kind of selfishness is basically right—as I mentioned earlier, self and the happiness of that self are our original right, and we have every right to overcome suffering—but selfishness that leads to no hesitation to harm another, to exploit another, that kind of selfishness is blind. Therefore, I sometimes jokingly describe it this way: if we are going to be selfish, we should be wisely selfish rather than foolishly selfish.

I feel that the moment you adopt a sense of caring for others, that brings inner strength. Inner strength brings us inner tranquility, more self-confidence. Through these attitudes, even though your surroundings may not be friendly or may not be positive, still you can sustain peace of mind. That much, according to my own little experience, I can tell you.

Expecting tranquility or peace of mind through money or through power is wrong. The ultimate potential to create peace of mind, a happy person, a successful and happy future, depends to a large extent on inner qualities. Of course, external facilities, such as money, are useful, we need them, but they are not the ultimate source or condition of inner peace.

Through inner disarmament we can develop a healthy mental attitude, which also is very beneficial for physical health. With peace of mind, a calm mind, your body elements become more balanced. Constant worry, constant fear, agitation of mind, are very bad for health. Therefore, peace of mind not only brings tranquility in our mind but also has good effects on our body.

With inner disarmament, now we need external disarmament. As I mentioned earlier, according to today's reality, there no longer is room for war, for destruction. From a compassionate viewpoint, destruction, killing others, and discriminating even against one's enemy are counterproductive. Today's enemy, if you treat them well, may become a good friend even the next day.

Also, bigger issues like overpopulation, environmental problems, and so forth are now beyond national boundaries. These are not questions of my nation's survival but of the survival of humanity. These bigger issues are our common responsibility to tackle. Compared to these problems, small, small things within ourselves are minor. Once all the bigger issues are solved, then there will be time to discuss—even, if necessary, to quarrel—among ourselves concerning these small, small things.

External disarmament is very, very important. Already, there is some movement. My dream is that one day the whole world will be demilitarized, but we cannot achieve this overnight. Also, we cannot achieve it without a proper, systematic plan; however, it is important to make the target clear. Even though it may take one hundred years, or fifty years, that doesn't matter. Establish a clear idea or clear target; then try to achieve it step by step. As a first step, we have already started with the elimination of antipersonnel mines and biological weapons. Also, we are already reducing nuclear weapons; eventually, there should be a total ban on nuclear weapons. This is now foreseeable; the idea of its possibility is approaching. These are great, hopeful signs.

Thus inner disarmament and external disarmament are needed. Then, as I mentioned earlier, problems always remain, we need some kind of humanistic way to solve problems: compromise. Sometimes I say that the twentieth century, which is my generation's century, more or less has been the century of bloodshed. Although a lot of achievements have taken place, in certain respects this period remains a century of bloodshed or a century of violence. But we humans—through difficult, painful experience—are, generally speaking, becoming more mature such that now we are talking about peace, about non-violence. These are becoming political forces, or political ideas. This is a very good sign.

The twenty-first century should be a century of dialogue. We, the present generation, have to picture the goal clearly and make preparation for a happier, friendly, and peaceful next century so that when my generation is ready to say good-bye, we can hand over a more hopeful world to the next fresh, broad-minded generation; then they will look after themselves. This is my feeling. Judging from various developments, it seems that in spite of some unhappy or painful conflicts here and there, the situation, in general, is getting better and better due to more awareness. Also, human thinking is becoming more open.

As a conclusion: it is very, very important to remain with hope and determination. If we lose hope and remain with pessimism, that is the greatest failure. In spite of difficulties, ah! remain with optimism—ah! these things change, can be overcome. Determination and hope are key factors for a brighter future. That much I wanted to share with you. If you agree, then try to think more on these topics, investigate them, and eventually implement them. If you feel these are too idealistic, not practical, then forget them! No problem.

Thank you.

Discussion Among the Participants

Jody Williams: Given the situation with Tibet and China, how do you apply your philosophy, which we have just heard—of hope, determination, compromise—to change between Tibet and China?

His Holiness the Dalai Lama: Hmmm. In fact, that was supposed to be a theme of my talk! Actually, I feel that, more or less, many people know about the Tibetan situation, and if I repeat it, then, of course, it is only painful information and distressing experiences.

But, let me say that since formal meetings with Chinese officials ceased in August, 1993, we have kept contact through other, more informal channels, and from the beginning of this year, the nature of that contact has become more substantive. For Chinese officials in Tibet, their main concern is day-to-day stability. If there are no demonstrations on the street, then they feel this is O.K. They are not much concerned about long-term consequences as a result of this present suppressive policy. Actually, this is counterproductive. In Beijing, naturally, there are various perspectives—some leaders are thinking in a more moderate or more serious way, and therefore, I think this is a time when it is better for me to be low-key. Let us see what new developments arise within the next few months.

When some of the recent Nobel Laureates, and also the representative of Aung San Suu Kyi, explained here about their nation's difficulties, a feeling of a little sadness arose in my mind. You can speak very freely, whereas I have to look from various aspects; so sometimes it is a little difficult. While I was hearing some of the Nobel Laureates express themselves freely, I felt, "I wish."

Anyway, about the Tibetan situation, I think there is a possibility to develop mutual trust; that's the key thing. Also, meeting person-to-person regularly and often is the best way to eliminate suspicion. One of the obstacles between the Chinese government and me is too much suspicion. Still, many people are really showing genuine concern and sympathy; I appreciate this very much.

From 1979 until 1986 I tried my best to solve these problems through direct communication with the Chinese government, but it did not materialize. The Chinese government formally or officially did not even admit that there is a problem about Tibet. The only problem, they said, was my return, and so they made a five-point proposal about my return. I told the Chinese government that this is not the real issue—the main issue is the six million Tibetan people, their right, their welfare, preservation of their culture, their spirituality. In the meantime, inside Tibet things got worse and worse. There was no other alternative except to appeal to the international community. Since then, the response year by year has really increased and is very, very encouraging. So, I want to take this opportunity to express my deep appreciation.

I want to make it clear that the solution must be found through direct communication with the Chinese government. I feel that there should not be any basis of suspicion since I am not seeking independence; I am seeking genuine autonomy, self-rule, because my main concern is the preservation of Tibetan culture as well as

Buddhist spirituality. This is of interest not only for the six million Tibetan people but also for the larger human community in that part of the world and, particularly, among the Chinese. Historically, there have been quite a number of Chinese following Tibetan Buddhism. Therefore, the preservation of the Tibetan Buddhist culture is also in the interest of the Chinese in the long run. Therefore, my aim or goal is very clear.

The Chinese government right from the beginning considered Tibet a unique case. That is what Chairman Mao and also Zhou Enlai made very clear to us: the Chinese central government does not consider Tibet to be like any other Chinese province—they said the Tibetan case is special. Also, the constitution of the People's Republic of China provides for self-rule or autonomy. In the Tibetan case, it provided for a Tibetan autonomous region as well as Tibetan autonomous counties and districts outside of the so-called Tibetan Autonomous Region. The problem is that this autonomy is not meaningful. I am seeking *genuine* autonomy. This means that foreign affairs and defense would be handled by the Chinese central government; Tibetans should have full authority for the rest.

Julian Bond: Your Holiness, you spoke of suspicion on both sides. What is the root of the suspicion on both sides?

His Holiness the Dalai Lama: With respect to the Tibetan side, I would cite a Tibetan saying, "Once you have been bitten by a snake, you will even fear the next time you see a rope." But basically, I believe the People's Republic of China is in the process of changing; that's definite. Year by year, things are better and better.

With respect to the Chinese government's side: naturally it is an authoritarian system. Right from the beginning, when we became refugees, the Tibetan community started to work for democratization; so, we can't stop the expression of Tibetan individuals or groups of Tibetans. People in the Tibetan refugee community here and there sometimes express their grievances or their resentment—there is a historical right for this. Then the Chinese government gets more suspicious. Are these expressions created by me, or does the Dalai Lama not fully control these things? I can't control them. Of course, once the things that we are seeking are clearly recognized by the Chinese central government—genuine self rule—then I can persuade the Tibetan community: "Ah! Now we are getting something. So, therefore, please don't carry on these kinds of demonstrations." Until that situation develops, I also find it difficult to convince the Tibetan refugee community that it should not carry on certain kinds of expressions. So I think this also is a basis of suspicion.

Questions from the Audience

Jeffrey Hopkins: The first question is for Your Holiness. How do you deal with Tibetan youth who are frustrated with oppression from the Chinese Communist government and turn to violence?

His Holiness the Dalai Lama: I always explain that violence is not the human way. I believe that, fundamentally, human nature is positive, gentle; therefore, the non-violent way is the human way. Also, whatever result we achieve through non-violence has no negative side effect. Through violence, even though we may get some kind of satisfaction, negative side effects are also incurred. Then, most importantly, whether we like it or not, we have to live side by side with the Chinese; thus, in the long future, generation to generation, in order to live happily, peacefully, it is extremely important, while we are carrying on the struggle, to accord with the principle of non-violence. Sometimes certain youths are a little frustrated; sometimes, we have had heated arguments.

But now I have other ammunition. We are receiving more and more support from the Chinese community, not only outside, but even in mainland China. Some writers, some thinkers, some educationists—although a small number, but growing—are expressing their solidarity, their sympathy, and their concern. And they are critical about the central government's policy. These are, I think, the result of our non-violent approach.

Jeffrey Hopkins: The next question is for President Arias. Can you please comment on capital punishment, a form of punishment used often in the United States.

President Oscar Arias Sánchez: There is not much I could say. In my country, we abolished capital punishment since 1888.

Bobby Muller: Could I jump in on that real quick? I'm going to Chicago next weekend, where an interesting meeting will be held. To that convention they've invited seventy-five people who were convicted of murder, placed on death row, and were subsequently found to be innocent. Think about that.

Betty Williams: I love the saying I heard quite a while ago: "Why do we kill people who kill people to prove that killing people is wrong?" To me, the death penalty is legalized murder.

President Oscar Arias Sánchez: This might sound very harsh—it's a hard line, but I use it from time to time with my friends in Washington: "In this country, it's murder to kill one person, but if you kill one hundred thousand, then it's foreign policy."

Jeffrey Hopkins: This is a question for Betty Williams. The topic of overpopulation has come up during this conference. What is your opinion with regard to how to reduce overpopulation?

Betty Williams: That's a question I am frequently asked. In countries where people are starving, before a woman can hear anything about birth control, you have to feed her belly. We are dealing with that problem the wrong way, because the only comfort that man and woman have is in the comfort of each other and the result of that is a child, but before that man or woman can hear anything you've got to say about overpopulating, you've got to feed them.

Jeffrey Hopkins: This is a question for Harn Yawnghwe. Could you please share with us the source of your openness and compassion toward a government that has caused your people such immense suffering.

Harn Yawnghwe: It comes from a belief that even the generals, even the people who are doing all these things, are human. They have families, they have children. Some of them may be doing it through ignorance, some of them may be doing it because they have been wrongly told. Of course, you may feel that the ones responsible, the generals, should know better, but they don't. Myself, I have also made mistakes. I have also had different convictions, which I thought were very right.

Jody Williams: Could I relate an anecdote about that? One of my closest friends had an extremely unpleasant encounter with two men who left her beaten and naked in the street. For many years, I had the greatest hope that I would run into them sometime and do the same to them, or worse. Then I got involved in trying to stop the violence in Central America, and watched what happened to people over time who only sought violent revenge against those who have done things to them or people they love. You become them. Violence does breed violence. It changes one's own being. It was only after many years of seeing that personally, that I realized that if I were to meet the two gentlemen in question, I would rather talk to them and ask them about their own humanity than do them harm and be like them.

Harn Yawnghwe: I agree. If you can't forgive a person for doing something, it hurts you more than it hurts them. It eats away and eats away and eats away; eventually you are nothing but bitterness.

Jeffrey Hopkins: This question is for Dr. Menchú Tum. Who has been the most influential person in your life?

Dr. Rigoberta Menchú Tum: Beyond the indigenous communities themselves, beyond the indigenous women that I have always known in my life, I have been very much inspired by Nelson Mandela. Not only have I been inspired by him, but I continue to be inspired. But I also have other idols. Martin Luther King: I have always been very, very positively impressed by his struggle against racism in the United States. And also Gandhi. And then also many, many people in Central America that I have known all my life who unfortunately lost their lives in the wars of the last decade.

Jeffrey Hopkins: The last question is for His Holiness. What do you think is the best way for Americans and the U.S. to help Tibet?

His Holiness the Dalai Lama: Among the public, especially among students, and also in both Houses of Congress, there is strong sympathy and support. As a reflection of the public's concern and the Congress's concern, the administration also is taking great interest and is addressing the Tibetan issue seriously. When President Clinton visited China, he personally spoke about the Tibetan issue. In general, it is helpful for the public to remind the world about the Tibetan issue. Then also, since there are many Chinese students here and many Chinese-American citizens, it is useful to make Tibetan culture—Tibetan Buddhist spirituality—known to them.

Last year, I visited Taiwan; mainly, of course, the trip was non-political and of a spiritual nature. Among the many Taiwanese Buddhists, some have a negative opinion, a little suspicion, or doubt about Tibetan Buddhism. As a result of my explanations, they gained a somewhat clearer awareness and understanding about Tibetan Buddhism such that now they want to study and to practice it. Similarly, among our Chinese brothers and sisters, there are many who do not know what Tibetan Buddhist culture is.

Now, year by year, more books, more materials, on Tibetan culture and Tibetan Buddhism are appearing—these also are helpful, toward making Tibetan culture and Tibetan Buddhism known among our Chinese brothers and sisters.

Dr. Rigoberta Menchú Tum: I did not want to end without saying that I want to reiterate what His Holiness the Dalai Lama has said: that all of our actions, all of our motivations, are for others, for young people, acting in society with institutions and with others, and also in the belief that human beings can change. We human beings can change. We were not born bad. We become involved in one or another negative action, but we were not born that way. It is very important to believe in us as a human species. We are bad, we human beings, but we can change.

And, finally, I really want to say, "Thank you, thank you," to the University of Virginia and "Thank you," to you and you [Nobel Laureates] for these two wonderful days that we have had here together; they have been unprecedented, really very unprecedented. We have all learned so very, very much, motivating all of us.

Betty Williams: Now, I'd just like to say something about acting locally. You see this little pin that we are wearing? It says "$8.00" on it. You've got people working on this campus for very, very low wages. It's time you changed that.

Julian Bond: Ladies and gentlemen, before I ask the university president, John Casteen, to come and close out the conference, two quick things. First, it has been a great, great honor and pleasure for me to have served in this role over the past two days. I was thinking, looking at the listing of the conference participants, that it had been my great pleasure to meet Ralph Bunche, who won the Prize in 1950; Chief Albert Lutuli, who won it in 1960; Dr. Martin Luther King, who won it in 1964; Henry Kissinger, who won it in 1973. And it was my great pleasure, just two weeks ago, to meet Nelson Mandela, a real thrill. I have been incredibly entranced with the opportunity to have sat next to, and to have been in the room backstage, overhearing conversations among all of the notables gathered at this table. It was a rare, rare privilege, and a great, great honor.

And now, it's my great pleasure to read a joint declaration from the speakers.

Nobel Peace Laureate Joint Declaration

November 6, 1998

WE, THE UNDERSIGNED, have gathered in Charlottesville to participate in a conference presented by the University of Virginia and the Institute for Asian Democracy on human rights, conflict, and reconciliation. We wish to use this opportunity to reaffirm our missions to the international community.

Whereas, the children of the world are oftentimes victims of conflict and require protection, we must establish safe havens for children of war and advance the cause of children's rights;

Whereas, the vast majority of arms sales are to non-democratic governments and scarce resources are devoted to education, housing, and health, we call upon all nations to adopt the International Code of Conduct on Arms Transfers and to dedicate their resources to erasing the gap between the world's rich minority and its poor majority;

Whereas, in order to find a peaceful resolution to the Tibet issue, we urge that the Chinese government enter into negotiations that will serve the interests of the Tibetan and Chinese peoples. Also, that these negotiations be conducted expeditiously, as an indication of China's good will and sincere intent;

Whereas, the U.N. General Assembly has adopted resolutions calling for upholding the will of the Burmese people as expressed in the 1990 elections and further calls for the State Peace and Development Council to enter into a substantive political dialogue with Aung San Suu Kyi and representatives of ethnic groups as the best means of promoting national reconciliation and democracy, we urge that the U.N. resolutions be implemented fully;

Whereas, the dignity of the indigenous peoples of the world continues to be marginalized, we must accept and respect other peoples, communities, and cultures, and integrate the mosaic languages, traditions, and peoples into the community of nations;

Whereas, the people of East Timor have the right to self-determination as recognized by several U.N. General Assembly and Security Council resolutions, we call for an internationally supervised referendum to determine their future political status;

Whereas, the world community has responded to the global landmine crisis with the Mine Ban Treaty, already signed by 133 governments and ratified by 49, we call upon the signatory states to ratify and non-signatories to join as soon as possible and all governments to expand their commitment to mine clearance and victim assistance;

We resolve that, it is our hope that this declaration will advance not only our own initiatives but bring about a more peaceful world. Moreover, we urge the international community to seek new ways of promoting justice, reconciliation, and peace in societies making the transition from repression to democracy and from conflict to civil societies under the rule of law.

Betty Williams, Northern Ireland (1976)

Archbishop Desmond Tutu, South Africa (1984)

President Oscar Arias Sánchez, Costa Rica (1987)

His Holiness the Dalai Lama, Tibet (1989)

Harn Yawnghwe, participating on behalf of
    Aung San Suu Kyi, Burma (1991)

Rigoberta Menchú Tum, Guatemala (1992)
José Ramos-Horta, East Timor (1996)
Jody Williams, United States (1997)
Bobby Muller, United States (1997), for
    the International Campaign to Ban Landmines

Concluding Remarks by John T. Casteen III

President of the University of Virginia

Ladies and gentlemen, I have come primarily to thank you for coming and to express to you the gratitude of this university, its faculty, its students, its staff members, the neighbors in this community—but also of an extended community that, by television, crosses this land and, we hope, reaches other lands—for both your presence and your thoughtful words. We are grateful to many people, and I would like to acknowledge some whose special efforts have made this occasion possible. Our own Jeffrey Hopkins, who was the force behind and the director of this event; Michele Bohana, the political liaison for the conference and the director of the Institute for Asian Democracy. I'd like to acknowledge, also, that two of our deans, the current dean of the College and Graduate School of Arts & Sciences, Mel Leffler, and his immediate predecessor, Ray Nelson, have worked tirelessly to make the event occur. I'd like also to acknowledge Bryan Phillips, a graduate student in the Department of Religious Studies, who has coordinated the conference, and to thank him specifically for hard work and for many hours coordinating the thousand and one details that have made the conference occur.

To the laureates, and to those speaking for their causes—José Ramos-Horta, Aung San Suu Kyi, Harn Yawnghwe, His Holiness the Dalai Lama, Bobby Muller, Oscar Arias Sánchez, Rigoberta

Menchú Tum, Bishop Desmond Tutu, Betty Williams, Jody Williams—these words: your idealism, your wisdom, your compassion, and your practical sense about the world in which we live, your dedication to helping those who cannot help themselves, together exemplify the highest aims of humanity and also of citizenship as practiced in the world community. For those things we thank you. Few of us who come to hear you accomplish so much or set our sights so high. You show us that the human spirit can, in truth, stand up to tyranny. That it can break the cycle of hatred and revenge. That it can repair the carnage of war. That it can champion the rights of those whose freedom has been stolen from them. You are the peacemakers of our time, revered by every people, by every religion. We see your strength and your courage as models for those whose lives you have touched in these short days. I want to acknowledge that those qualities of yours are special contributions to education as we practice it here and in universities around the world.

In many ways, it is, perhaps, appropriate that this conference convenes here, in a place that proclaims that it is dedicated to the illimitable freedom of the human mind. You have told us, and we know, that in the real world freedom is often all too vulnerable, that freedom needs its champions, and that tolerance and love are virtues to be nurtured and taught. The events of this century have challenged the optimism and the capacity for the improvement of human nature that led to the establishment of institutions like this one. Your work and this event in this place have, perhaps, restored some of the faith implicit in the creation of universities dedicated to the illimitable freedom of the human mind. Your lives are arguments that humankind is capable of making ethical progress. Your presence here perhaps reminds each of us that we have both the ability and the duty to combat—in our minds and in our hearts, in every town, on every continent where it appears—the failure to recognize the commonality of humanity. We believe that this conference has succeeded. We believe that what has been discussed and determined here will make a difference in the lives of individuals, and in world dialogue for the possibility of peace and hope, and reconciliation.

Certain common threads run through the dialogue of these two days. Each of you has, in some way, exhorted us to individual action. Both words, "individual" and "action," matter. We must transform ourselves as individuals, before we can think of transforming the world. We must come to see ourselves as actors, not as observers, or merely consumers of information. Sentiment alone is not sufficient; instead, the obligation is to make conscience manifest, as each of you has done.

The other common theme is the central place of love and forgiveness in any vision of a better future. You have told us to work to increase the fund of compassion in the world, to acknowledge the humanity of humankind, to make the gift of forgiveness no matter how terrible the events that have come before.

So these may be the charges that we take away from this place: to recognize our responsibility, but also our power, as individual persons to turn that recognition to fruitful action and to conceive that action out of a sense of love and forgiveness. With this encouragement and these directions, perhaps more of us will have the vision, the courage, to intercede in the cycle of hatred and injustice. By your examples and your words, we may be able to determine how to make those things happen.

My profound gratitude to Jeffrey and to the organizers and participants in the event, a notable occurrence in American education, a notable occurrence in this institution. Let us take from these days a sense of hope and a sense of commitment, and a sense of the commonality of human concerns.